Britain's Best Afternoon Tea

© Automobile Association Developments Limited 2005. The Automobile Association retains the copyright in the current edition © 2005 and in all subsequent editions, reprints and amendments to editions.

www.theAA.com

To contact us
Advertising: advertisementsales@theAA.com
Editorial: lifestyleguides@theAA.com

The contents of this publication are believed correct at the time of printing. Nevertheless, the Publisher cannot be held responsible for any errors or omissions or for any changes in the details given in this guide or for the consequences of any reliance on the information it provides. This does not affect your statutory rights.

Assessments of AA inspected hotels are based on the experience of the Hotel Inspectors on the occasion of their visit(s) and therefore descriptions given in this guide necessarily dictate an element of subjective opinion which may not reflect or dictate a reader's own opinion on another occasion. We have tried to ensure accuracy in this guide but things do change and we would be grateful if readers would advise us of any inaccuracies they may encounter.

Ordnance Survey This product includes mapping data licensed from Ordnance Survey ® with the permission of the Controller of Her Majesty's Stationery Office.
© Crown copyright 2005. All rights reserved. Licence number 399221.

Maps prepared by the Cartography Department of The Automobile Association.
Maps © Automobile Association Developments Limited 2005.

Typeset by Keenes Repro, Andover
Printed and bound by Graficas Estella, S.A, Navarra, Spain

Editor: Jane Gregory
Writers: Julia Hynard, Denise Laing

Front and Back Cover photos sourced from AA World Travel Library, by photographers: Jon Wyand; Richard Ireland; Tony Souter; Wyn Voysey; Pete Bennett.

Images on pages 1,2,10,11,14,15,17,18 courtesy of The Tea Council and text on pages 6,7,8,10,11,14,15,16,17,71,116,167 courtesy of The Tea Guild

A CIP catalogue record for this book is available from the British Library

ISBN-10: 0 7495 4674 3
ISBN-13: 978 0 7495 4674 8

Published by AA Publishing, a trading name of Automobile Association Developments Limited, whose registered office is Fanum House, Basing View, Basingstoke, Hampshire RG21 4EA. Registered number 1878835.

A02578

CONTENTS

How to use the guide

The guide is divided into countries: England, Scotland, and Wales.

Each country is listed in county order, and then in approximate alphabetical town/village location within each county.

There is a county map on page 19 to help you locate counties within Britain. In the England section, counties are indicated at the top left or right side of each page.

The tea shops and tea rooms in this guide with this symbol in their entry are all members of The Tea Guild and have been inspected and approved by The Tea Council's inspectors.

AA Stars and Rosettes
The hotels in this guide have been inspected by the AA under the nationally recognised Star classification schemes, agreed between the AA, VisitBritain and the RAC, and enabling you to make your choice with confidence. Rosettes are awarded by the AA for food.

For a full explanation of these ratings and awards please see pages 12 & 13

Finding the Town
If you know which town you are looking for, refer to the index at the back of the guide. Towns are listed alphabetically, with their page number and establishments in or closest to the town. Within a town or village, establishments are listed approximately alphabetically.

The Example Tea Room
Genuine warm hospitality coupled with home from home comforts

1 — ☎ 01234 567899 🖷 01234 567898
🄴 e-mail@address.uk
🆆 www.lovely.com

2 — Map ref 6 - TQ40

3 — LANCASTER, LA6 1XX
2m off B6254 Carnforth - Kirkby Lonsdale.

4 — ☕ Open 10am-4pm; Tea served all day Closed Sun, 25 Dec; Set tea price(s) £5.50 - £10; Seats 45; No credit cards; No Smoking; No Dogs; Parking 12

5 — *T*his charming building dates in part from the 18th century.The conservatory, where tea is served, is an impressive Victorian structure, with palms and a fountain. Afternoon tea consists of a selection of finger sandwiches, freshly baked scones with clotted cream and preserves, tea bread and assorted pastries. Lady Anne's Tea goes further, with English muffins and gateaux.

RECOMMENDED IN THE AREA — **6**
Lancaster; Morecombe; Blackpool

❶ *Contact Details*
Telephone and fax numbers, e-mail and website addresses are shown as provided by the establishments.
Please Note - Website Addresses These are included where they have been supplied by the establishment and lead you to websites that are not under the control of The Automobile Association Developments Ltd. The Automobile Association Developments Ltd has no control over and will not accept any responsibility or liability in respect of the material on any such website. By including the addresses of third party websites the AA does not intend to solicit business.

❷ *Map Reference*
The map refers to the town or village. The map page number refers to the atlas at the front of the guide, and is followed by the two-figure National Grid Reference. To find the location, read the first figure horizontally and the second figure vertically within the lettered square. Maps locating each establishment can also be found on the AA website, www.theAA.com

❸ *Address and Directions*
The full postal address of each establishment is given, followed by brief directions.

❹ *Establishment Details*
Where the establishments have given us up-to-date information, the following details are included:
- Prices for set teas
- Number of seats
- Smoking restrictions (see below)
- Opening times, and times when tea is served
- Days or times of year when closed
- Whether dogs are allowed
- Whether parking is provided
- Room numbers and prices for hotels

❺ *Description*
The description of the establishment includes information about the tea room or lounge and the type of food available.

❻ *Recommended in the Area*
We asked the establishments to tell us about places to visit in their area which they recommend to their guests.
The AA Days Out Guide, available from bookshops or the AA website, may also prove useful in finding things to do in the area.

Local Specialities
At the start of each county in England, and also for Scotland and Wales, we have highlighted traditional tea time delicacies that you should look out for.

Hotel Listings for London, Scotland and Wales
We have included a listing of hotels that have told us they offer afternoon tea to non-residents at the end of the London, Scotland and Wales sections.

www.theAA.com
The AA website gives details of all AA recommended accommodation, including all the places to stay listed in this guide.

www.tea.co.uk
The Tea Council website gives details of all Tea Guild Members.

Recipes
This year we have included some recipes in the guide. These have all been provided by the establishments and have not been tested by the AA or The Tea Guild.

Complaints
Readers who have any cause to complain are urged to do so on the spot. This should provide an opportunity for the proprietor to correct matters. If a personal approach fails, readers should inform AA Lifestyle Guides, Fanum House, Basingstoke RG21 4EA. The AA does not however undertake to obtain compensation for complaints.

Smoking Restrictions
Smoking restrictions for hotels are given for the tea lounge only and not for the establishment as a whole (unless otherwise stated). If smoking regulations are of importance to you please make sure that you check the exact details with the establishment when booking.

What is The Tea Council?

The Tea Council is a non-profit organisation representing the interests of the major tea producing countries and the UK tea trade. The Council acts as a spokesperson for the tea industry on a wide range of topics, and is also involved in promoting the health benefits of tea drinking.

One of its most important initiatives is The Tea Guild, an organisation that encourages the tradition of excellence in tea brewing, and reflects the importance of taking tea as an enjoyable social ritual.

The Tea Guild

The Tea Guild was founded in 1985, after an independent survey, commissioned by The Tea Council, found that out of the thousands of beverage serving outlets across the country, few were serving tea to the standards desired by The Tea Council.

The Guild was set up to provide recognition to those outlets meeting these high standards.

Membership of The Tea Guild is strictly by invitation only. When a tea room is interested in becoming a member, they are visited by an incognito tea taster. If that establishment complies with The Tea Council's high standards (see page 8) they are then invited to become a member.

Tea Guild members are able to benefit from the resources and reputation of The Tea Council , and from publicity and promotions organised by the Council.
They also receive automatic entry into the annual search for *Top Tea Place of the Year* or the *Top London Tea Place* – both competitions attract extensive coverage in the press.

What defines the ideal tea shop or tea room?

The ideal catering outlet that The Tea Council looks for to join The Guild must focus particularly on tea. They must serve good quality tea, offer a wide selection of tea to cater for all tastes and they must brew and serve these teas well. The outlet must also offer an atmosphere in which customers feel welcome, comfortable, relaxed, and are treated with care and courtesy.

This sort of outlet might be one of the following:

• a traditional tea shop or tea room in a country cottage

• a traditional tea shop in a town centre in, for example, a Georgian house or a Victorian shop

• a hotel lounge that serves morning coffee, lunchtime snacks, cocktails etc., and usually a set afternoon tea with sandwiches, scones and pastries

• a restaurant that doubles as a tea room during the afternoon and offers good teas throughout the day and after dinner

• a tea area attached to or part of an antiques market, garden centre, or craft and art gallery

• a modern tea bar, similar to a coffee bar but serving mainly tea, and which may offer take-away tea as well as pots of tea to drink in the shop

• an oriental-style noodle or dim sum restaurant that serves an excellent range of Chinese teas as well as other black, green and flavoured teas from around the world.

The Crockery and Teapots Used by Tea Shops

The teapots, cups and saucers, general crockery and cutlery chosen by individual tea places can vary enormously and should link with the overall style, theme and atmosphere of the venue. A top quality tea room may offer different brewing and drinking vessels according to the types of tea they serve.

Teapots

Pots made from certain materials are not suitable for the successful brewing of tea. These are aluminium, pewter, enamel, uncoated iron and plastic. They may taint the tea or emit undesirable substances into the infusion.

The best teapots are made from porcelain, bone china, glazed stoneware, unglazed Chinese red earthenware, silver and glass. These lose heat slowly from the outside and maintain a good temperature inside. When the visual effect of the brewing of the leaves and the colour of the liquor is required, glass is excellent. The size and shape of the teapot is very important. It is essential that the correct amount of tea and water are used in each pot and that the leaves have enough room to move around in order to absorb water and release their colour and flavour into the water.

Cups and Saucers

There is no doubt that porcelain and bone china make the best teacups. They keep the tea hot, they are more elegant and they are easy to lift.

But depending on the style and theme of a teashop, different materials may be used. However, the heavy stoneware and pottery often used for catering tablewares allow the tea to cool more quickly than porcelain and bone china and are generally less acceptable to most people.

The shape of cups is also important. A wide top allows the tea to cool faster while taller, narrower shapes are excellent for piping the aroma of the tea. This is important with some of the fine China green and oolong teas.

Cups, mugs or bowls?

For traditional British tea drinking, cups and saucers are best. For oriental teas (oolongs and green teas from China and Japan) little bowls or tall straight-sided cups with no handles are culturally correct and add an interesting and colourful element to the tea drinking experience.

The Tea Council's Awards

The Tea Council rates establishments who are members of The Tea Guild by matching their performance against strict criteria. A summary of these is given below.

Tea shops, tea rooms and tea lounges in London hotels are awarded a number of 'teacup' symbols from one to five, depending on how well the judges consider they have upheld the high standards of The Guild and the tradition of tea.

Hygiene and Décor
Cleanliness and décor are obviously very important. In addition to The Tea Council's exacting standards of hygiene, there should be no dust, stains on teacloths, or anything that might be distasteful to a paying customer. Any food preparation areas in view must be clean, with raw and cooked foods kept separately.

Crockery
Tea should be served in a pot, with enough tea/tea bags to ensure an appropriate strength of brew. All pottery or china must be in good condition with no cracks, chips or stains. Stainless-steel milk and water jugs are not favoured. If loose-leaf tea is served, a strainer or infuser should always accompany it. There should be a different strainer for each type of tea (so that one type is not being strained through another).

Staff Attitude and Efficiency
Staff should be friendly and well presented, having a reasonable knowledge of the different varieties of teas on offer, and service should be efficient and attentive.

Variety of Tea
Different varieties of tea should be listed on the menu. There should be a good range of teas from the main growing countries, and both leaf and bag tea should be on offer.

Staff Knowledge of Tea
Staff should know the difference between the teas available and be able to advise customers depending on their tastes, and also give advice about whether the tea chosen should be taken with milk or lemon.

Milk
To cater for all tastes and diets, full fat, semi-skimmed and skimmed milk should be available, with semi-skimmed milk being offered as the norm. A slice of lemon should also be available if required.

Sugar
Lumped sugar is best – in a covered sugar bowl if possible. Tongs should be provided where sugar lumps are served; sweeteners should also be available.

Cakes and Foods
Fresh, tasty home-baked foods are looked for, a wide selection on offer, served attractively and stored hygienically.

Overall Ambience and Value for Money
Afternoon tea should be treated as an 'experience'; therefore customers should be offered a relaxing, interesting and enjoyable environment in which to enjoy it.

Top Tea Place Winner
Ollerton Watermill Tea Shop, Ollerton, Nottinghamshire

In its charming location on the edge of Sherwood Forest, the Watermill Tea Shop has been justly popular for more than 10 years. Sisters-in-law Kate and Ellen Mettam opened the tea room after their husbands decide to restore the mill, which dates back to 1713 and has been in the Mettam family since 1921. Kate and Ellen are proud of their reputation for upholding The Tea Council's exacting requirements regarding knowledge and quality of tea, together with standard and presentation of food; and we congratulate them on winning this year's Top Tea Place award.

Top London Tea Place Award
The Conservatory at The Lanesborough

The award for Top London Tea Place is eagerly sought after and hotly contested. Afternoon tea at a top London hotel is a very special treat, and the Conservatory's staff successfully demonstrated their awareness of this important consideration, as well as their confident knowledge of tea and willingness to offer advice when requested. The tea served was always bright and hot, and ranged from deliciously fragrant to brisk and full of character; service in the peaceful garden setting was of an exceptional standard, and this combined with the presence of a pianist to transform the experience into an unforgettable 'occasion'.

The Tea Guild's Award of Excellence 2005

More than thirty of the tea shops and tea rooms in the guide have been chosen to receive the annual Tea Guild Award of Excellence. Look out for the special symbol in their entries.

Abbey Cottage Tea Rooms, New Abbey, Dumfries
Badgers Café & Patisserie, Llandudno, Conwy
Bettys Café Tea Rooms, Harrogate, North Yorkshire
Bettys Café Tea Rooms, Ilkley, West Yorkshire
Bettys Café Tea Rooms, Northallerton, North Yorkshire
Bettys Café Tea Rooms, York, North Yorkshire
Bird on the Rock Tearoom, Clungunford, Shropshire
The Bridge Tea Rooms, Bradford-on-Avon, Wiltshire
Cemlyn Restaurant & Tea Shop, Harlech, Gwynedd
Charlotte's Tea House, Truro, Cornwall
Claris's, Biddenden, Kent
The Corn Dolly, South Molton, Devon

De Grey's, Ludlow, Shropshire
E Botham & Sons, Whitby, North Yorkshire
Flying Fifteens, Lowestoft, Suffolk
Gilbert White's Tea Parlour, Selborne, Hampshire
Greystones 17th Century Tea Room, Leek, Staffordshire
Haskett's Tea & Coffee Shop, Dorking, Surrey
The Hazelmere Café & Bakery, Grange-over-Sands, Cumbria
Kind Kyttock's Kitchen, Falkland, Fife
Little Bettys, York, North Yorkshire
The Marshmallow, Moreton-in-Marsh, Gloucestershire
Muffins Tea Shop, Lostwithiel, Cornwall
New Village Tea Rooms, Penrith, Cumbria
Northern Tea Merchants, Chesterfield, Derbyshire
Searcy's at the Pump Room, Bath, Somerset
Shepherd's Tearooms, Chichester, West Sussex
Tea on the Green, Danbury, Essex
The Tea Room, Edinburgh
The Tea Shop, Wadebridge, Cornwall
The Tea Tree Tea Rooms, Winchelsea, Sussex
Trenance Cottage Tea Room & Gardens, Newquay, Cornwall
The Willow Tearoom, Glasgow

Tea for Health

The latest research has shown that drinking your cuppa provides you with positive health benefits. The antioxidants, hydrating properties, caffeine and fluoride found in tea mean that you need never feel guilty about reaching for the teapot.

The Tea Council and The Royal Society of Medicine recently launched a £1.5M 'tea4health' campaign, urging Britons to drink four cups of tea per day to gain maximum health benefits. In support of this campaign, The Tea Council has published the results of a comprehensive study demonstrating the health benefits associated with drinking tea, including robust evidence that, like fruit and vegetables, black tea contains powerful antioxidants, which can help to prevent heart disease and some cancers.

A panel of experts, including internationally renowned nutritionists and biochemists, have also identified tea drinking as being hydrating rather than dehydrating; also, due to its relatively low caffeine content, drinking tea is mood enhancing yet has no negative effect on sleep quality or duration. Tea is even advantageous for dental health, through both its naturally occurring fluoride and its antibacterial properties. Some major food retailers are backing the campaign, with plans to relocate their tea to the fruit and veg aisle.

The **tea4health** campaign specifically targets young people, who currently drink less than half as much tea as the over 50s. The Tea Council's research has shown that although young women are increasingly drinking tea rather than coffee, many are shunning tea in flavour of water – which they find a chore, rather than something they enjoy. The **tea4health** campaign aims to dispel the myths associated with tea drinking, and makes the definitive recommendation that drinking at least four cups of tea a day provides vital health benefits.

Drinking tea is part of Britain's culture. Most people enjoy a tea-break, whether at work or at home; and with the cost working out at about 3p per cup, there is no comparison with fashionable coffee shop concoctions costing around £2 each.

As a nation, we are already drinking 165 million cups per day, which equates to just under three cups each. The **tea4health** campaign is intending to increase that to at least four cups per day, to ensure that the maximum health benefits are gained.

So, now you can relax with that fourth cup of tea, knowing that you're looking after your health.

Health Facts

• Approximately 40% of the nation's fluid intake today will be tea.

• Tea without milk has no calories. Using semi-skimmed milk adds around 13 calories per cup, but you also benefit from valuable minerals and calcium.

• Tea with milk provides 16% of daily calcium requirement in 4 cups. Tea contains some zinc and folic acid.

• Tea with milk contains Vitamin B6, Riboflavin B2 and Thiamin B1.

• Tea is a rich source of the minerals manganese, essential for bone growth and body development, and potassium, vital for maintaining body fluid levels.

• The average cup of tea contains less than half the level of caffeine found in coffee. One 190ml cup contains only 50mg.

• Tea is a natural source of fluoride and delivers 45% of your daily requirement if you drink three to four cups per day.

• Only 11% of the UK's water supply has fluoride added.

• Green and black teas are from the same plant, *Camellia sinensis*, and contain similar amounts of antioxidants and caffeine.

For further information on tea and health contact:

The Tea Council Ltd
9, The Courtyard
Gowan Avenue
London
SW6 6RH

Tel: 020 7371 7787
Fax: 020 7371 7958
or visit www.tea4health.com

AA Classifications and Awards

The AA inspects and classifies hotels, guest houses and restaurants with rooms. Establishments applying for AA quality assessment are visited on a 'mystery guest' basis by one of the AA's team of qualified accommodation inspectors. Inspectors stay overnight to make a thorough test of the accommodation, food and hospitality offered. On settling the bill the following morning they identify themselves and ask to be shown round the premises. The inspector completes a full report, making a recommendation for the appropriate level of quality (see below). The establishments in this guide have been recommended by AA inspectors for their excellent hospitality, accommodation and food.

AA Star Classification

If you stay in a one-star hotel you should expect a relatively informal yet competent style of service and an adequate range of facilities, including a television in the lounge or bedroom and a reasonable choice of hot and cold dishes. The majority of bedrooms are en suite with a bath or shower room always available.

A two-star hotel is run by smartly and professionally presented management and offers at least one restaurant or dining room for breakfast and dinner, while a three-star hotel includes direct dial telephones, a wide selection of drinks in the bar and last orders for dinner no earlier than 8pm.

A four-star hotel is characterised by uniformed, well-trained staff with additional services, a night porter and a serious approach to cuisine. Finally, and most luxurious of all, is the five-star hotel offering many extra facilities, attentive staff, top quality rooms and a full concierge service. A wide selection of drinks, including cocktails, is available in the bar, and the impressive menu reflects and complements the hotel's own style of cooking.

The AA's Top Hotels in Britain and Ireland are identified by red stars. These stand out as the very best and range from large luxury destination hotels to snug country inns. To find further details see the AA's website at www.theAA.com

AA Rosette Awards

Out of around 40,000 UK restaurants, the AA awards rosettes to around 1,800. The following is an outline of what to expect from restaurants with AA Rosette Awards.

Two Rosettes

- The best local restaurants
- Higher standards
- Better consistency
- Greater precision apparent in the cooking.
- Obvious attention to the quality and selection of ingredients.

About 40% of restaurants have two Rosettes.

Three Rosettes

- Outstanding restaurants demanding recognition well beyond local area.
- Selection and sympathetic treatment of highest quality ingredients
- Timing, seasoning and judgement of flavour combinations consistently
- Excellent intelligent service and a well-chosen wine list

Around 10% of restaurants with Rosettes have been awarded three.

Four Rosettes

- Cooking demands national recognition

Dishes demonstrate:
- intense ambition
- a passion for excellence
- superb technical skills
- remarkable consistency
- appreciation of culinary traditions combined with desire for exploration and improvement.

Around fifteen restaurants have four Rosettes.

One Rosette

- Excellent local restaurants stand out in their local area
- Food prepared with care, understanding and skill
- Good quality ingredients

Of the total number of establishments with Rosettes around 50% have one Rosette.

Five Rosettes

- Cooking stands comparison with the best in the world
- Highly individual voices
- Breathtaking culinary skills
- Setting the standards to which others aspire

Around six restaurants have five Rosettes.

The Tradition of Tea

Around 40% of what we drink daily in Britain - apart from tap water - is tea, which makes it the nation's favourite drink. At times of crisis our first resort is the kettle, for there's nothing like the comfort of a freshly brewed cuppa. We've been drinking tea for over 300 years and drink an average of three cups a day. Whatever the occasion, wedding or wake, everything stops for tea and the inevitable gathering around the steaming pot. Tea is not, however, native to the British soil, so how did this love affair begin?

Chinese Roots

Legend has it that tea drinking began in China more than 5,000 years ago, when the Emperor Shen Nung, a man of serious scientific principles, decreed that all drinking water should be boiled for reasons of hygiene. One day, while travelling far from home, the court stopped to boil up some water, dried leaves from a bush fell into the pot and the inevitable occurred.

Tea-drinking spread throughout Chinese society, and in 800 AD the first book about tea was written by a man called Lu Yu, brought up as an orphaned child by Buddhist monks. Through many years of observation he recorded methods of tea cultivation and preparation, which led to the creation of a tea service, informed by his Zen Buddhist approach, which was carried by Buddhist priests to imperial Japan.

The 'Father of Tea' in Japan was Yeisei, a Buddhist priest who brought tea seeds into the country from China. He believed that tea was an aid to religious meditation, and in Japan the association between tea and Zen Buddhism remains. The service of tea was elevated to a high art in Japanese society, inspiring a complex and stylised ritual and even its own form of architecture.

The European Experience

A Portuguese Jesuit, Father Jasper de Cruz, was the first European to write about tea with any real authority in 1560. He was a missionary on the Portuguese navy's first trading trip with China when he encountered the exotic beverage. Prior to this, earlier European travellers had been uncertain as to what tea was actually for, and seemed under some misapprehension that it should be boiled and eaten as a vegetable. Holland at this time had close affiliations with Portugal and also entered into the tea trade.

When tea first arrived in Europe in 1610, its immense cost made it the preserve of the wealthy, but as its popularity grew, the price fell and it was swept up in the prevailing passion for all things Oriental. The first mention of milk being added to the brew was observed by the Marquise de Seven in 1680, though the popularity of tea in France was relatively short lived.

Tea came to Russia in 1618, as a gift from the Emperor of China to the Tsar. The Russians developed a taste for the stuff, but they traded overland by camel - tea for furs - over a long and perilous route.

Tea In Britain and The Colonies

Britain was the last of the three great seafaring nations to join the Chinese and East Indian trade routes. Under a charter granted by Elizabeth I, East India Company ships reached China in 1637, but it was not until 1644 that any tea dealing was recorded. Sailors returning from the Far East introduced tea to the London coffee houses and by 1700 there were more than 500 such establishments serving the drink.

King Charles II grew up in exile in France and Holland, returning to re-establish the monarchy in 1660. He married the Portuguese Infanta Catherine de Braganza in 1662, and both were confirmed tea drinkers. Catherine brought chests of tea from Portugal as part of her dowry and the royal couple established the tea habit in Britain as a social and family ritual. During the 18th century, tea drinking spread to wealthy American colonists. Anger over the high taxes England levied on tea turned to protest with the Boston Tea Party in 1773, an event that triggered the American colonies' fight for independence.

When tea was first taken up in the grander British homes, it was served at the end of the evening's entertainment, before the ladies went to bed. From the 1730s, London's pleasure gardens at Vauxhall and Ranelagh began serving tea, to round off an evening of dancing and fireworks, and soon tea gardens were a popular phenomenon all over the country.

The British Tradition

The tradition of afternoon tea is credited to Anna, Duchess of Bedford, who in the early 1800s had the idea of serving tea with a little something to eat to stave off the pangs between lunch and dinner. This quickly became the custom in polite society, and an enjoyable occasion for friends and family to get together.

Tea did not become widely available to working people until the mid to late 19th century, with the importation of cheaper tea grown in India and Sri Lanka and the advent of the clipper ships, which speeded up transportation. The burgeoning temperance movement also necessitated a cheap alternative to the usual beer or ale.

For labourers, a cup of tea meant a break from work, the reviving comfort of a hot drink and the stimulus of the caffeine content. The high tea of the ordinary folk was different from the afternoon tea of high society. It was the main meal of the day for those who could not afford a proper cooked meal, comprising bread, meats, cakes or pastries, served with a good strong cuppa.

The country's first tea shop was started in 1864 by the manageress of the Aerated Bread Company, when the company directors permitted her to serve refreshments to favoured customers. Demand for the service grew, sparking a trend for similar establishments across Great Britain. These did much to liberate the lives of women, as it was considered perfectly proper for a woman to meet friends in a tea shop without the imposition of a chaperone. Today, with our Guide, we honour this unnamed woman as the founder of a fine tradition proudly upheld by a grateful nation.

What is Tea?

The making and drinking of tea is a deeply embedded national tradition and many of us would struggle through the day without its comforting, thirst-quenching and reviving properties, yet how much do we know about this exotic plant from faraway lands?

All the tea drunk in the world is made from the leaves of the same evergreen, tropical plant, a member of the Camellia family (*Camellia sinensis*), which has shiny green pointed leaves and was originally indigenous to both China and India. In its wild condition, tea will grow into a tree some 30 metres high, but under cultivation the plant is kept at around a metre for ease of picking. The bush is trained to grow into a fan shape, with a flat top called a plucking table, and it takes between three and five years to reach maturity. Only the top two leaves and a bud are picked from the sprigs on the plucking table, and the rate of re-growth will depend on the altitude at which the bush is grown. A tea bush at sea level will replace itself more quickly than a bush grown at a higher level where the air will be cooler. The bushes are picked, generally by hand, every 7-14 days. A skilled tea 'plucker' can pick up to 35 kilograms in a day, which will produce 7.5-9 kilograms of processed black tea. Most factories produce black tea, where the leaf is dried, broken, fermented and dried or fired again. For green tea, the withered leaf is steamed and rolled before drying, to stop the veins in the leaf from breaking, thus preventing oxidisation or fermentation. Tea grows best in a warm, humid climate where there is at least 100 centimetres of rain a year. It likes a deep, light, acidic and well-drained soil. Appropriate conditions might be found at sea level or up to 2,100 metres above sea level. The flavour of the tea will depend on the type of soil the plant is grown in, the altitude and the climate. The processing of the leaf and the blending of leaves from various places will also affect the character of the final product.

There are more than 1,500 teas to choose from, and tea is grown in around 30 different countries around the world, including:

China

For centuries China tea was the only tea known to the Western world and was extensively used in blends. China remains a major tea producer, but is best known now for speciality teas such as Lapsang Souchong, Keemun, the Oolongs and green teas.

India

The tea plant is indigenous to the Assam area of India, but the first tea grown commercially in the country was brought as seeds and cuttings from China. In 1835 The East India Company established experimental tea plantations in Assam, and by the 1840s Indian tea was being exported to England on a regular basis. Tea picking in Assam and Darjeeling is seasonal, and Darjeeling is known as the Champagne of teas. Nilgiri, grown high in the hills, is not dissimilar to the teas of Sri Lanka.

Indonesia

The Dutch East India Company began the tea trade in these Southeast Asian islands around 200 years ago, and tea from Indonesia, India and Ceylon dominated the market for black tea until World War II, The industry did pick up after the war, and these days the light, fragrant Indonesian teas are largely used for blending.

Kenya

Kenya is a very fertile country, with a climate that allows tea to be picked all year round. Tea production in Kenya is believed to date from 1903, when two acres of tea was planted using imported seeds from India. Today Kenya is the largest exporter of black tea in the world, and over 50% of tea imported into the UK is from Kenya.

Malawi

The first African country to experiment with tea planting, Malawi has been trading tea since the 1870s, and was also the first African country to adopt the cloning or cuttings method to refurbish tea plantations. Though it may not be as well known as the speciality names, Malawian tea is featured in many well-known British blends. Like other East African teas, the product is bright and colourful with a reddish tint.

Sri Lanka

Sri Lanka, formerly known as Ceylon, was well known for its coffee in the 19th century, but in the 1870s the Ceylon coffee crops were decimated by coffee rust fungus. Many planters followed the example of Scotsman James Taylor who had successfully planted the island's first tea estate in the hills above Kandy. Sri Lanka produces high, medium and low-grown teas, each with its own character.

Tanzania

Tea production really took off between the wars under the British flag. The country produces high, medium and low-grown tea, each with its own characteristics, but still discernibly East African.

Zimbabwe

Tea was originally grown under the influence of the British. The first irrigated tea estate was established here, a necessity in Zimbabwe, as the low annual rainfall is only about half that usually required for tea production.

Useful Information

Fire Precautions and Safety

Many of the hotels listed in the guide are subject to the requirements of the Fire Precautions Act of 1971, and should display details of how to summon assistance in the event of an emergency at night.

Codes of Practice

The AA encourages the use of The Hotel Industry Voluntary Code of Booking Practice in appropriate establishments. Its prime objective is to ensure that the customer is clear about the price and the exact services and facilities being purchased, before entering into a contractually binding agreement. If the price has not been previously confirmed in writing, the guest should be handed a card at the time of registration, stipulating the total obligatory charge.

The Tourism (Sleeping Accommodation Price Display) Order 1977 compels hotels, motels, guest houses, farmhouses, inns and self-catering accommodation with four or more letting bedrooms to display in entrance halls the minimum and maximum prices charged for each category of room. This order complements the Voluntary Code of Booking Practice.

Dogs

Establishments which do not normally accept dogs may accept guide dogs. Some establishments that accept dogs may restrict the size and breed of dogs permitted and the rooms into which they may be taken. Please check the conditions when booking.

Children

Restrictions for children may be mentioned in the description. Some hotels may offer free accommodation to children when they share their parents' room. Please note that this information may be subject to change without notice and it is essential to check when booking.

County Index

The county map shown here will help you identify the counties within each country. The England section of the guide has the county names in the panel at the edge of each page. To find towns featured in the guide use the map pages which follow, and the index at the back of the book. The numbers below refer to the numbers on the map.

England

1	Bedfordshire
2	Berkshire
3	Bristol
4	Buckinghamshire
5	Cambridgeshire
6	Greater Manchester
7	Herefordshire
8	Hertfordshire
9	Leicestershire
10	Northamptonshire
11	Nottinghamshire
12	Rutland
13	Staffordshire
14	Warwickshire
15	West Midlands
16	Worcestershire

Scotland

17	City of Glasgow
18	Clackmannanshire
19	East Ayrshire
20	East Dunbartonshire
21	East Renfrewshire
22	Perth & Kinross
23	Renfrewshire
24	South Lanarkshire
25	West Dunbartonshire

Wales

26	Blaenau Gwent
27	Bridgend
28	Caerphilly
29	Denbighshire
30	Flintshire
31	Merthyr Tydfil
32	Monmouthshire
33	Neath Port Talbot
34	Newport
35	Rhondda Cynon Taff
36	Torfaen
37	Vale of Glamorgan
38	Wrexham

County Map

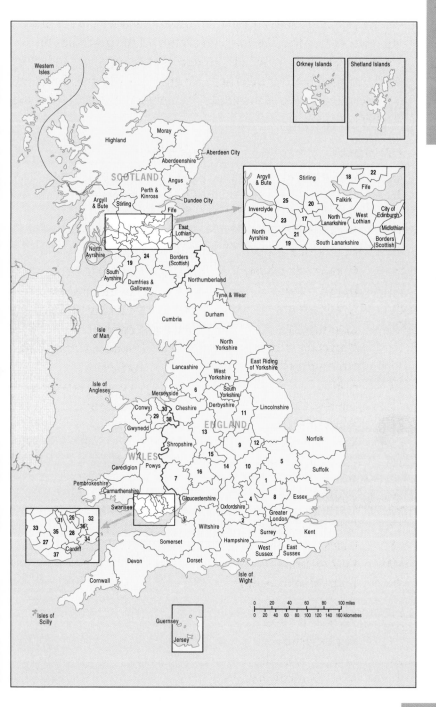

County & Country Index

KEY TO ATLAS PAGES

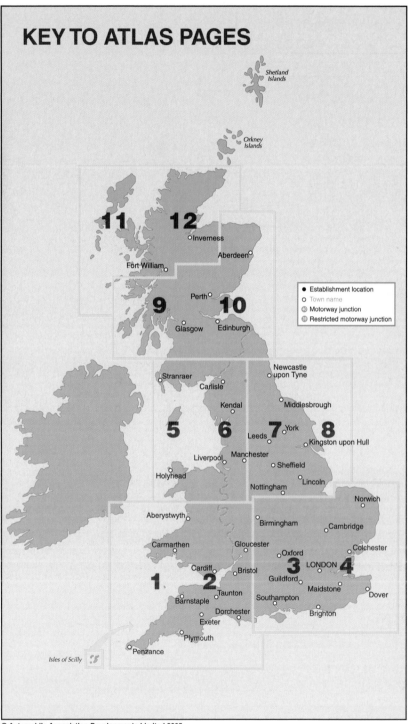

Shetland Islands

Orkney Islands

11   12

Inverness

Aberdeen

Fort William

9   10

Perth

Glasgow   Edinburgh

- ● Establishment location
- ○ Town name
- ⑩ Motorway junction
- ㉚ Restricted motorway junction

Newcastle upon Tyne

Stranraer

Carlisle

Kendal

Middlesbrough

5   6   7 York   8

Leeds

Liverpool   Manchester   Kingston upon Hull

Holyhead

Sheffield

Nottingham   Lincoln

Norwich

Aberystwyth

Birmingham   Cambridge

Carmarthen   Gloucester   Colchester

Cardiff   Bristol   Oxford   3 LONDON 4

1   2   Guildford   Maidstone

Taunton   Southampton   Dover

Barnstaple   Dorchester   Brighton

Exeter

Isles of Scilly   Plymouth

Penzance

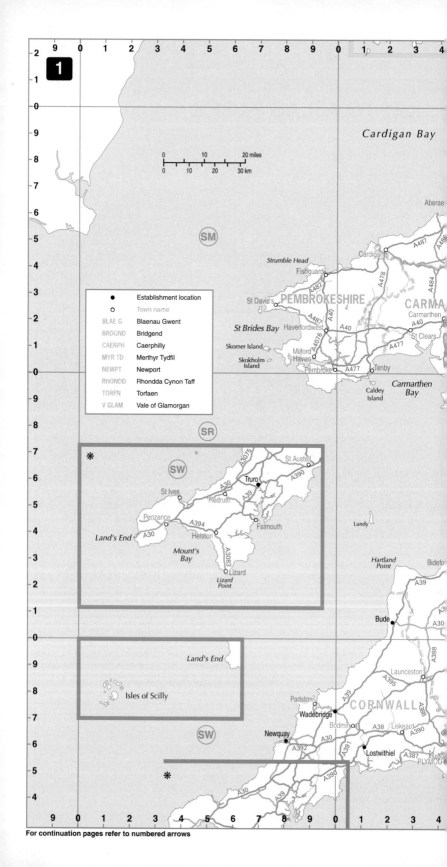

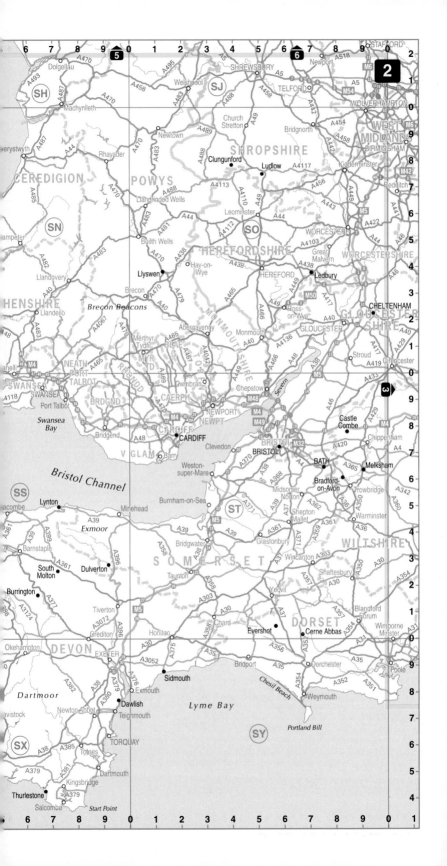

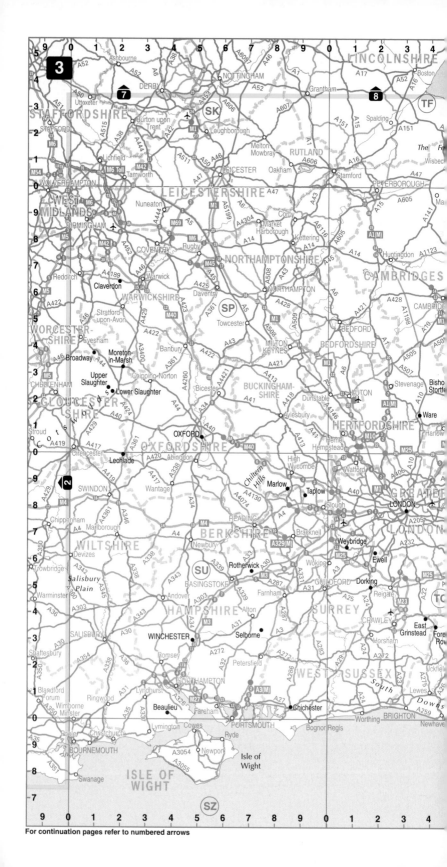

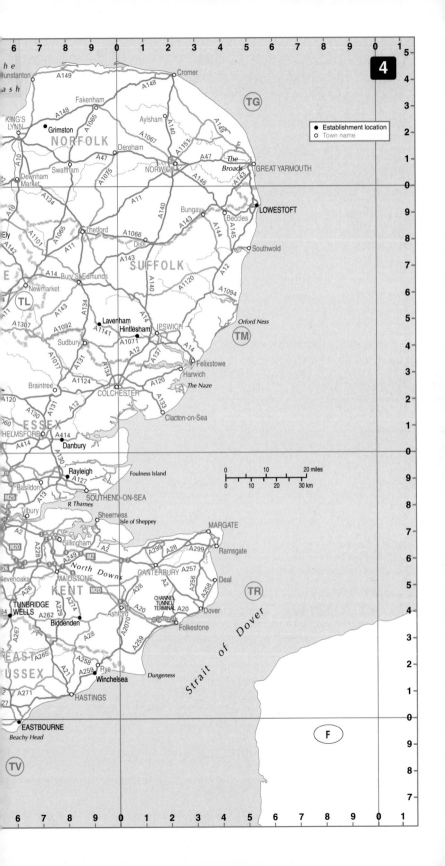

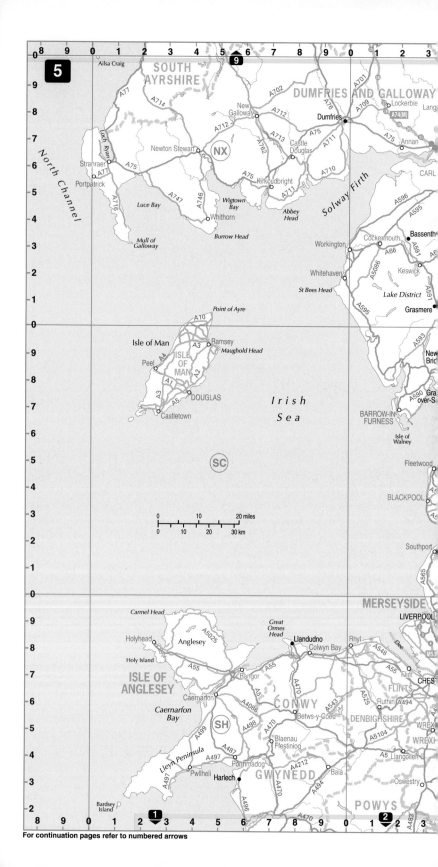

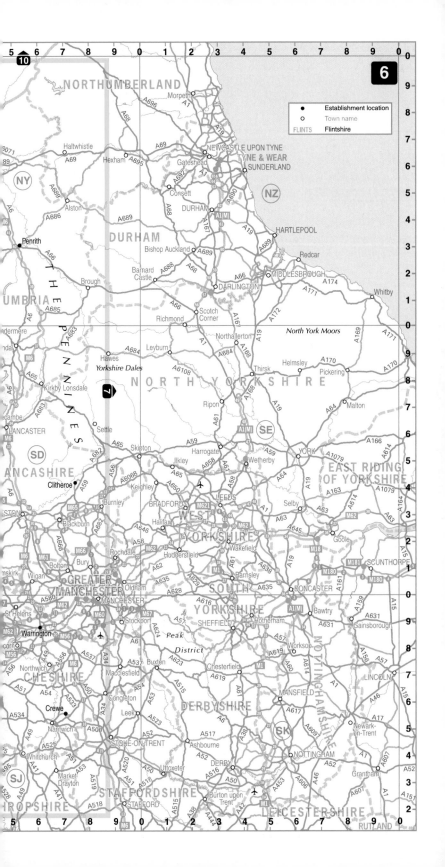

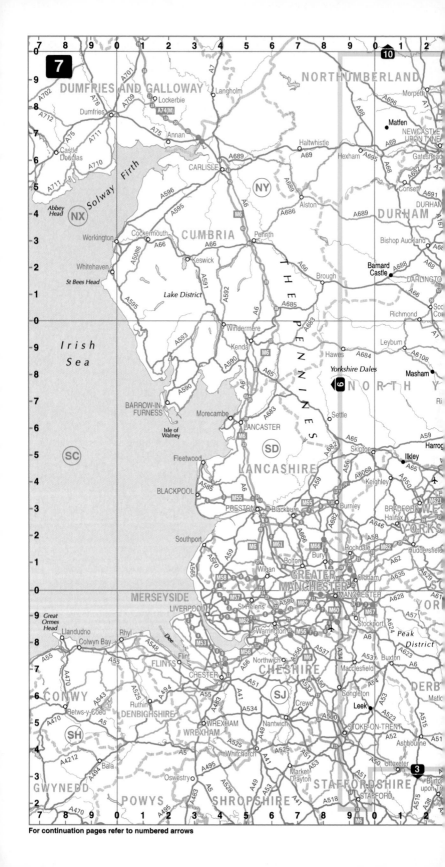

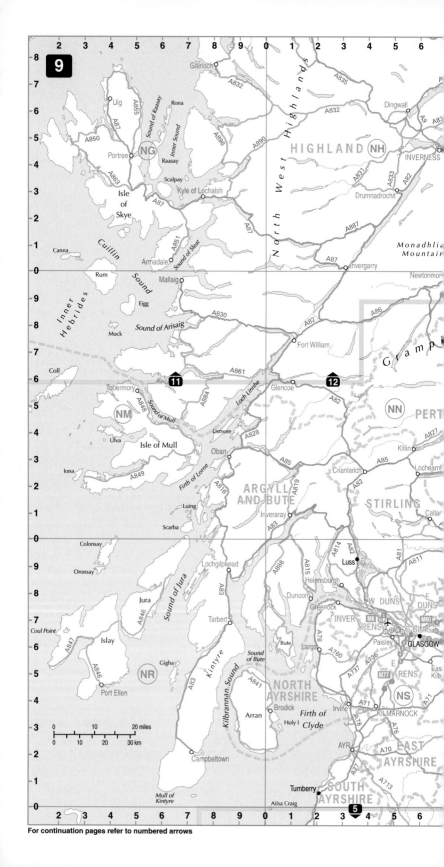

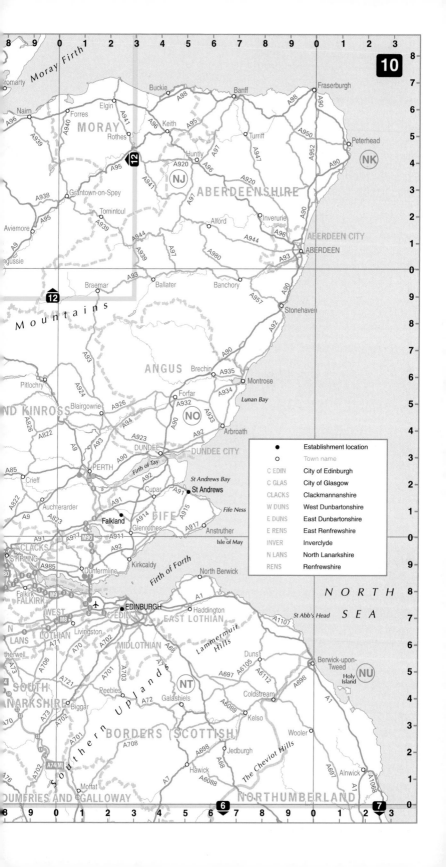

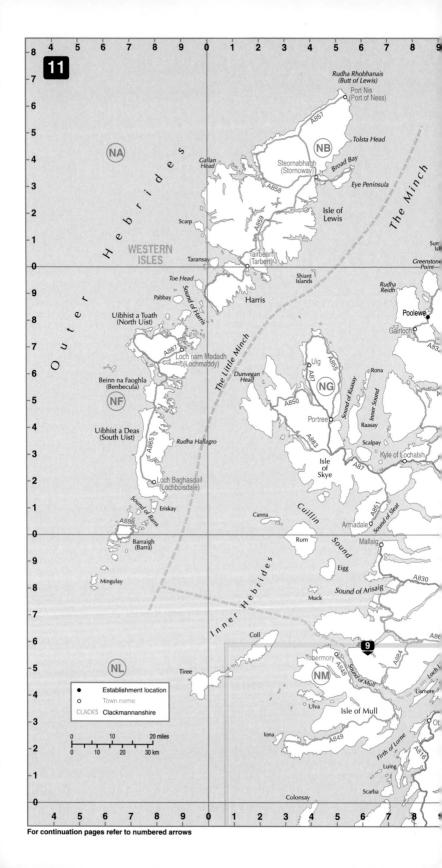

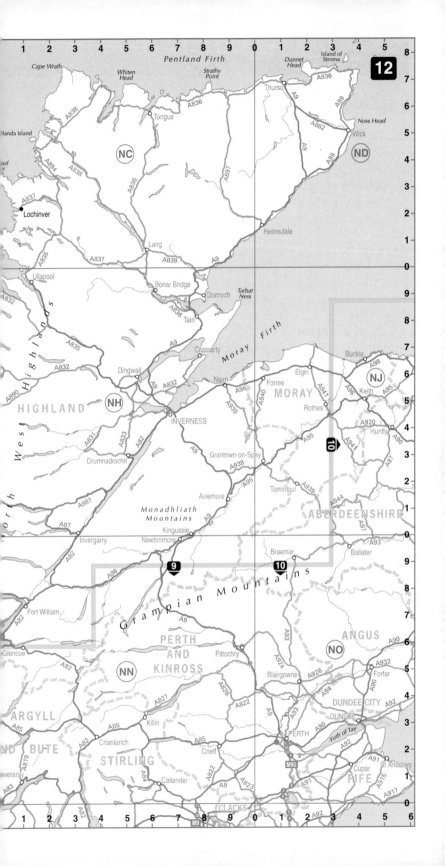

Bristol

Sugar to sweeten our teatime specialities has long been associated with the City of Bristol. The importation of sugar from the Caribbean during the era of the iniquitous slave trade, from 1698, laid the foundation for a major sugar processing industry in the city.

Bristol is also home to a renowned cream sherry, bottled in 'Bristol blue', the flagship product of Harveys, a company established in 1796. The great English classic, sherry trifle, is believed to date from the late 16th century, beginning as a simple syllabub-type concoction and developing over the years to its many-layered complexity of sherry-soaked sponge, fruit, custard and cream.

*B*ristol Marriott Royal Hotel ★★★★ ◎◎◎
Home-made pastries served in a luxurious hotel drawing room

☎ 0117 925 5100
📠 0117 925 1515
✉ bristol.royal@
   marriotthotels.co.uk
🌐 www.marriott.co.uk/brsry

Map ref 2 - ST57

College Green, BRISTOL, BS1 5TA
Next to cathedral.
🍴 Open daily; Tea served 2pm-6pm;
Set tea price(s) from £8.95; Seats 50;
Air con; Dogs allowed on request;
Parking 200 (charged)
🛏 242 Rooms; S £85-£155,
D £130-£155

Splendid Victorian surroundings blend with stylish modern luxury to create an ideal setting for afternoon tea at this superb hotel. Easy to find, it stands next to the cathedral in the city centre; once inside, the positive first impressions are heightened by polished mahogany and marble, and bright chandeliers. Tea is served amid lavish comfort in the Club Lounge and the Drawing Room, and there are also tables outside for warm afternoons. Home-made pastries and cakes created by the award-winning kitchen's speciality chef are served at tea time, and those seeking a more filling meal will find a choice of sandwiches and wraps.

RECOMMENDED IN THE AREA
Bristol Hippodrome; Bristol Old Vic; SS Great Britain

Buckinghamshire

Buckinghamshire is known for its rich and fertile farmland, and was once one of London's main suppliers of milk. Famously home to the Aylesbury duck, long believed to be the most delicious in Britain (although many birds referred to as such these days are cross breeds), Buckinghamshire was also once well known for plums, grown to make prunes, and also to provide dye for the Luton hat factory.

Olney is famous for its pancake race, where local women make pancakes on the first ring of the church bell and race on the second, dressed in aprons and headscarves. They have to toss the pancake three times.

Buckinghamshire Stokenchurch Pie is a good supper dish, made with macaroni, hardboiled eggs, and any leftover cooked meat. Mix the macaroni with the meat, place half in a pastry-lined pie dish, add the eggs, and then cover with the rest of the meat and a pastry lid and bake for half an hour.

*D*anesfield House Hotel & Spa ★★★★ ◉◉

Victorian mansion house with a 65 acre estate overlooking the Thames

☎ 01628 891010
𝟡 01628 890408
✉ sales@danesfieldhouse.co.uk
🌐 www.danesfieldhouse.co.uk

Map ref 3 - SU88

Henley Road, MARLOW-ON-THAMES, SL7 2EY
M4 junct 8/9 or M40 junct 40, A404, A4155
Marlow, follow Henley signs for 3m, under
footbridge, hotel on left.
🍵 Open daily; Tea served 3pm-6pm;
Closed 25-26 Dec; Booking recommended at
weekends; Set tea price(s) Cream Tea £9.50,
Afternoon Tea £14.50, Champagne Tea
£19.50; Seats 60; Air con; Guide dogs only;
Parking 100
🛏 87 Rooms; S £175-£355, D £220-£355

Spectacular views across the River Thames are afforded from this country house hotel, which is set in 65 acres of grounds high up in the Chiltern Hills. Impressive public rooms include the Grand Hall, panelled Oak Room restaurant and The Orangery. There are three set teas to choose from: the cream tea, afternoon tea or champagne tea. The fullest option comprises finger sandwiches, scones with jam and clotted cream, rich fruit cake, shortbread, dainty cakes and pastries, along with a glass of champagne, bucks fizz or champagne cocktail. Lavender scones are a house speciality, as are interesting sandwich fillings such as tuna with pickled ginger and wasabi.

RECOMMENDED IN THE AREA
Windsor Castle; Hell Fire Caves; Dashwood Estate

Danesfield Lavender Scones

Recipe supplied by
Danesfield House Hotel & Spa
(page 35)

Makes between 8 and 12 scones

Ingredients

8oz (225g) self raising flour
pinch of salt
2oz (55g) butter
1oz (25g) caster sugar
5fl oz (150ml) milk
1/2 handful (2g) lavender seeds

Method

Preheat oven to gas mark 7/425°F/220°C.
Mix together flour, salt and lavender seeds and rub in butter.
Stir in sugar and then milk to make a soft dough.
Turn out onto a floured surface and knead very lightly.
Pat out to a round 3/4in (2cm) thick and cut into rounds using a
2in (5cm) scone cutter. Lightly knead the rest of the dough together and
cut into more scones to use it all up.
Brush tops of scones with a little milk.
Bake for 12–15 minutes until well risen and golden.
Cool on a wire rack.
Serve with good quality jam and clotted cream.

Cambridgeshire

Sturdy, comforting College Pudding originates from Cambridge, and 19th-century students also tucked into 'cream darioles' – almond pastry tartlets with a rich custard filling. An unusual fruit named for the city is the Cambridge gage – related to the greengage and with a pleasant flavour at once sharp and sweet, it is good for cooking or bottling. Further afield is Ely, the cathedral city of the Fens; eels were historically vital to the economy here, and are still served as a local delicacy. Vegetables thrive in the fertile soil of the Fens, and local recipes make excellent use of another Ely speciality – celery, which is delicious baked in spices and seasoned cream, topped with fresh breadcrumbs.

Peacocks

A friendly tea shop not far from the Cathedral

☎ 01353 661100
✉ tea@thepeacocks.co.uk

Map ref 4 - TL58

65 Waterside, ELY, CB7 4AU
Down hill from Cathedral, overlooking River Great Ouse and Slipway, between Waterside Antiques Centre and Babylon Gallery.
Owner(s): George Peacock & Rachel Lemkov
🍵 Open 10.30am-4.30pm Wed-Sun; Tea served all day; Closed Mon, Tue & one month in winter (usually Jan); Set tea price(s) Cream Tea £5, Full Afternoon Tea £10; Seats 30 + 24 outside; No smoking; Dogs allowed in garden only

George Peacock and Rachel Lemkov add a little extra to the traditional tea room experience. Light meals such as Norfolk ham salad and home-made cakes are available all day, including Rachel's scones, served with Cornish clotted cream. The choice of teas is remarkable, with 40 listed, from the usual suspects to many more unusual varieties. Try something different – maybe the Venetian Te Ciocclato if you have a taste for chocolate, or a cherry scented Japanese sencha. The Special Afternoon Tea includes finger sandwiches, scones with a choice of jam (strawberry, raspberry or 'jam of the week') and a choice of cake.

RECOMMENDED IN THE AREA
Ely Cathedral; Waterside Antiques Centre; River Great Ouse walks and boat trips

Cheshire

Cheshire cheese is the oldest of our cheeses with a slightly salty tang from the soil of the Cheshire salt marshes. Cheshire makes a delicious Welsh rarebit and is also very good in potted cheese. Traditionally, the cheese is grated, mixed with butter and spice, moistened with a splash of sherry or brandy, and beaten thoroughly until smooth. The mixture is firmly pressed into small pots, sealed with melted butter and kept in the fridge. Potted cheese is delicious spread on toast for tea. A speciality of the county town is Chester pudding – a pastry case with a frangipane-type filling and a meringue topping.

*T*he Chester Grosvenor & Spa ★★★★★ ◉◉◉

Great location in the heart of the city

RECOMMENDED IN THE AREA
Roman walls & amphitheatre; Stately homes and gardens; Chester Cathedral; Chester Zoo

☎ 01244 324024
✆ 01244 313246
✉ hotel@chestergrosvenor.com
⊛ www.chestergrosvenor.com

Map ref 5 - SJ36

Eastgate, CHESTER, CH1 1LT
On Eastgate in city centre.
♟ Open daily; Tea served 3pm-5pm; Closed 25-26 Dec; Booking advisable; Set tea price(s) Grosvenor Tea £18.50, Indulgent Grosvenor Tea £27.50; Seats 119; Air con; Guide dogs only; Children over 12 only; Parking 500
🛏 80 Rooms, D £180-£695

A Grade II listed building dating back to 1865, the hotel's traditional black and white timber frontage is quite deceptive; the interior is luxuriously elegant and stylish. The Library is the setting for tea, and has an intimate, comfortable atmosphere with large sofas to relax into while awaiting your tea. The Grosvenor Tea features a selection of finger sandwiches, fruit and plain scones with clotted cream and strawberry jam, followed by French pastries and fancies. You can go a step further with the Indulgent Grosvenor Tea and have strawberries and rosé champagne as well. Chester is a lovely city, with plenty of things to do and see, so be sure to do some exploring before you sit down to tea.

Crewe Hall ★★★★ ◉

Magnificent and welcoming, the perfect place for tea

☎ 01270 253333
📠 01270 253322
✉ crewehall@
marstonhotels.com
🌐 www.marstonhotels.com/
cgi/booking/b.pl

Map ref 5 - SJ75

Weston Road, CREWE, CW1 6UZ
M6 junct 16, A500 to Crewe, last exit at rdbt onto A5020, 1st exit at rdbt to Crewe. Hotel approx 100 metres on right.
🍽 Open daily; Tea served 2pm-5.30pm; Sun 3pm-5.30pm; Booking recommended; Set tea price(s) High Tea £9.95, Cream Tea £13.95, Champagne Tea £18.50; Seats 30; No smoking; Guide dogs only; Parking 140
🛏 65 Rooms; S £183-£383, D £233-£433

A former stately home, once the seat of the Earl of Crewe, standing in large grounds. Some breathtakingly beautiful features, including the chapel and the pantry, simply have to be seen, and there are guided historic tours for the curious. A Victorian architect extended the original Jacobean pile, and the Grade I listed building offers gracious reception rooms that were seemingly designed for afternoon tea. In the ornate Sheridan lounge you can try the light tea of sandwiches and speciality tea or coffee, the high tea – sandwiches, cakes, warm scones with clotted cream and jam, or the full Crewe Tea (booking only).

RECOMMENDED IN THE AREA
Little Moreton Hall; Stapeley Water Gardens; The Potteries

The Park Royal Hotel ★★★★

A welcoming hotel with a good lounge menu

☎ 01925 730706
📠 01925 730740
✉ parkroyal@qhotels.co.uk
🌐 www.qhotels.co.uk

Map ref 5 - SJ68

Stretton Road, Stretton, WARRINGTON, WA4 4NS
M56 junct 10. Take A49 towards Warrington. Hotel 200 yards on R.
🍽 Open daily; Tea served 8.30am-10.30pm; Set tea price(s) £6.70; Air con; No dogs; Parking 542
🛏 142 Rooms; S £115, D £125

Travellers on the M56 can take heart as they approach Warrington, and allow themselves a detour for a highly profitable couple of hours. Their targeted destination is this comfortable modern hotel, where the spacious public rooms offer an ideal opportunity for refreshment. The lounge bar menu provides a tantalising choice of food throughout the day, from starters and main courses to tasty snacks and light meals. Should your visit occur in the afternoon, the tea menu will surely appeal: you can enjoy the full works, with a pot of tea or a cup of speciality coffee, or if that seems overwhelming, just a toasted teacake or crumpet instead.

RECOMMENDED IN THE AREA
Arley Hall & gardens; Trafford Shopping Centre; Blue Planet Aquarium

County Durham

Oats are a traditional staple of the north-eastern counties, from the days before wheat was much used in these parts, and oat cuisine is still reflected in the region's recipes.

Durham pikelets are a kind of pancake popular for tea. They are made from a batter mixture of flour, buttermilk and bicarbonate of soda, fried and served hot with butter and jam.

Monthly farmers' markets flourish within the county at Barnard Castle, Darlington, Durham, Stanhope and Sedgefield, and are good places to check out the local specialities, including home-made cakes and bread.

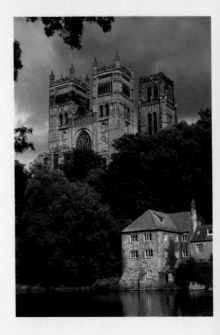

*T*he Market Place Tea Shop

Tasty teas and lunches at reasonable prices

☎ 01833 690110

Map ref 7 - NZ01

29 Market Place, BARNARD CASTLE, DL12 8NE
Owner(s): Robert Hilton
☕ Open 10am-5.30pm Mon-Sat,
Sun 2.30pm-5.30pm (Mar-Oct);
Closed 24 Dec-7 Jan; Set tea price(s);
Seats 42; Smoking area available

A charming tea shop, full of character with its 17th-century flagstones, bare stone walls and open fireplace. In previous lives it was a pub, and a gentleman's outfitters kitting out the local farm workers. Despite these rustic surroundings, tea is served in silver teapots by uniformed waitresses, and accompanied by a tempting list of goodies: meringues filled with cream and strawberries, Yorkshire curd cheesecake, fruit tarts and scones might appear on the daily-changing menu. Savoury dishes include home-made steak pie with vegetables, and prices are reasonable. The upstairs Artisan shop sells chinaware, glassware, prints and original paintings.

RECOMMENDED IN THE AREA

The Bowes Museum; Raby Castle; Barnard Castle; High Force waterfall

Cornwall

Clotted cream has to be the teatime treat most closely associated with this part of the world. It has a very high fat content and is simply divine served with scones or with another local favourite, Cornish splits. These are soft buns raised with yeast, split and filled with jam and cream.

Saffron was introduced to Britain in the 14th century and soon became a popular flavouring. Crocuses were cultivated in Essex to meet the demand for saffron, which is harvested from the flower's stigma. By the early 15th century the industry in Essex was finished, but saffron continued to arrive from abroad at the Cornish ports. Thus saffron cake, bread and bun recipes remained part of the Cornish tradition, but were generally reserved for special occasions because of the extravagant nature of the critical ingredient. It takes 150,000 flowers to produce one kilogram of dried saffron!

The Cornish pasty, the tin miner's highly portable staple, is a perennial favourite, which finds continuing appeal with today's eat-on-the-move generation. The crisp ginger biscuit known as the Cornish Fairing is also still widely available, originally made to munch on fair days. Seafood is another regional speciality, and crab cakes, crab soup or a fresh crab sandwich are a delight at any time.

*T*he Old Rectory Farm Tearooms

A 13th-century farmhouse just ten minutes from spectacular Cornish cliffs

☎ 01288 331251

Map ref 1 - SS20

Rectory Farm, Morwenstow,
NEAR BUDE, EX23 9SR
*Turn off A39 at sign to Morwenstow
and follow signs for approx 4m.*
Owner(s): Jill Savage
☕ Open Easter-end Sep daily; Tea
served 11am-5pm; Out of main
season may close in bad weather,
please telephone to check; Booking
possible; Set tea price(s) Cream Tea
£5.25, Speciality Cream Tea £5.70;
No credit cards; Seats 30; No
smoking; No dogs; Parking 30

*D*ating back to 1296, when it belonged to an order of monks, this working farmhouse is (not surprisingly) full of atmosphere. Heavy oak beams salvaged from wrecked ships, ancient flagstone floors worn by countless feet, and large open fireplaces with blazing logs on cold days, all help to make a visit here memorable. Speciality teas such as Gunpowder, Chai and China Oolong appear on a long list of drinks. There is a good selection of food too – everything is cooked on the premises using fresh local ingredients wherever possible. Try a Cornish cream tea with huge scones and Cornish clotted cream, or a Ploughman's with a good selection of Cornish cheese, chutney and coleslaw. Also cakes, soups and pasties. Vegetarians and children catered for. Some produce and crafts on sale.

RECOMMENDED IN THE AREA
*Cornish Coastal Path; Church of St John the Baptist
(900AD); Killarney Springs Adventure Park*

*M*uffins Tea Shop

An award-winning tea shop serving varied meals and teas

☎ 01208 872278
✉ info@muffins32.fsnet.co.uk
🌐 www.muffins32.fsnet.co.uk

Map ref 1 - SX16

32 Fore Street, LOSTWITHIEL,
PL22 0BN
*Off A390, on main street of Lostwithiel
near the church.*
Owner(s): Keith & Lindsay Southgate
☕ Open Tue-Sat 10am-5pm, plus
Sun & Mon in Jul & Aug; Tea served all
day; Booking possible; Set tea price(s)
Cream Tea £3.75, Full English Tea
£6.50; Seats 24; No smoking;
No dogs

*I*n summer a lovely walled cottage garden is just the place for afternoon tea. At other times the light and spacious tea shop with its pretty tablecloths and pine furniture is a magnet for tourists. Parts of Lostwithiel date from the late 13th century, but Muffins has moved with the times and serves a variety of tasty meals throughout the day, based where possible on fresh local produce. The Cornish Cream Teas are hard to beat, with their delicious Trewithen clotted cream and strawberry jam, or you can try the famous home-made muffins. You can buy food and gifts to take home.

The Tea Guild's Award
of Excellence 2005

RECOMMENDED IN THE AREA
*The Eden Project; Lanhydrock (National
Trust); Restormel Castle (English
Heritage)*

Cornish Honey Muesli Bars

Recipe supplied by Old Rectory Farm Tearooms
(page 42)

Ingredients

6oz (175g) self raising flour
8oz (225g) margarine
6oz (175g) rolled oats
4oz (110g) demerara sugar
2 tablespoons clear Cornish honey
2 tablespoons golden syrup
2oz (50g) apricots, chopped
2oz (50g) raisins

Method

Preheat oven to gas mark 4/350°F/180°C.
Rub flour and margarine together, stir in oats, sugar, honey, syrup, raisins
and apricots, and mix well.
Put mixture into a shallow prepared non-stick pan, press well down
and bake for 25 minutes until golden brown.
Remove from oven and cut into 12 squares; leave for 10 minutes and
transfer to a cooling rack, until completely cold.

*H*eadland Hotel ★★★★ ⊛

Simply stunning coastal setting and incredible views

☎ 01637 872211
🖷 0 637 872212
✉ otfice@headlandhotel.co.uk
🌐 www.headlandhotel.co.uk

Map ref 1 - SW86

Fistral Beach, NEWQUAY, TR7 1EW
*From A30, follow signs for Newquay via
A3058/A3059/A392. On edge of Newquay, follow
signs for Fistral Beach. Hotel at end of headland
on right.*
Owner(s): Mr & Mrs J Armstrong
🍽 Open daily; Tea served 10am-10pm (low
season midweek, to 7pm); Closed 25 -26 Dec;
Group bookings possible; Set tea price(s) Cornish
Cream Tea £5.50; Seats 100 -150 in brasserie, bar
& lounge; Air con; Parking 100
🛏 104 Rooms

*S*urrounded on three sides by the Atlantic Ocean, this magnificent Victorian hotel (described as 'the largest and most palatial in the west of England' when it was built) seems to rise from the sea as you approach it. The dramatic location (the hotel sits on its own promontory) has made it a popular choice as a film location; Roald Dahl's *The Witches* was filmed here, amongst others. The views across the sea and down to Fistral Beach really are amazing. Staff are very friendly and welcoming, and high standards are set throughout the hotel. The Sand Brasserie or the Lounge are the setting for tea, or sit out on the terrace when it's warm – the views, again over Fistral beach, are a really wonderful backdrop for a traditional Cornish Cream Tea. There is also a daily selection of plain and sweet pastries, muffins, cookies and cakes. At weekends a pianist plays in the Lounge during the evening.

RECOMMENDED IN THE AREA
*Fistral Beach surfing; Eden Project; National
Maritime Museum; Tate St Ives*

Trenance Cottage
Tea Room & Gardens

A highly acclaimed cottage tea room where the emphasis is on quality, local, home-made fare

☎ 01637 872034
✉ robert@trenance-cottage.co.uk
🌐 www.trenance-cottage.co.uk

Map ref 1 - SW86

Trenance Cottage, Trenance Lane,
NEWQUAY, TR7 2HX
*From town centre take Edgcumbe Avenue
into Trevemper Road. Trenance Cottage
opposite boating lakes.*
Owner(s): Bob & Judy Poole
🍵 Open Apr-Oct 10.30am-5pm; Tea served
all day; Closed Nov-Mar; Booking possible;
Set tea price(s) Cream Tea £4.95; No credit
cards; Seats 30 + 90 outside; No smoking;
Dogs allowed outside only

Dating back some 200 years, Trenance Cottage is believed to have been one of the earliest licensed tea gardens in the area. In more recent years, proprietors Bob and Judy Poole have extensively renovated the property while focusing on the tea room tradition, with background music from the 1920s through to the 50s to strike a nostalgic note. Conveniently close to Newquay Airport, they also offer bed and breakfast accommodation in three rooms. Trenance Cottage is a member of the Tea Council Guild of Tea Shops, and the menu lists a wide choice of teas and tisanes. Other house specialities are fresh local crab and smoked mackerel, locally grown strawberries, home-baked Cornish pasties, cream teas with local clotted cream, and locally made strawberry conserve. Light lunches, including home-made soup, ploughman's and Welsh rarebit, are served, plus a range of Cornish wines, beers and ciders during licensing hours. Some parking space is provided, and it is usually easy to park in adjacent roads. Preserves, tea and biscuits can be bought to take away. Dogs are permitted outside. Trenance Cottage has won many awards over the years including The Tea Guild's Top Tea Place 2001 and 2002, and The Tea Guild Award of Excellence 2003 and 2004.

The Tea Guild's Award of Excellence 2005

RECOMMENDED IN THE AREA

Gannell River Walks; Coastal paths; Newquay Zoo

Ginger Parkin

Recipe supplied by Trenance Cottage Tea Room and Gardens (page 45)

Ingredients

5oz (150g) Stork margarine
6oz (175g) black treacle
4oz (110g) soft brown sugar
2 standard eggs
1 tablespoon water
8oz (225g) self raising flour
2 teaspoons ground ginger

Method

Put margarine, black treacle, sugar and water into a saucepan and heat gently, and stir until margarine has melted.

Sieve flour and ginger into the mixing bowl, pour on melted ingredients, and beat until thoroughly mixed.

Add eggs and beat again, then pour into a greased and lined oblong bread tin. Bake in an electric oven for approx 50 minutes at gas mark 3/325°F/170°C (fan oven 160°C). Turn out onto a wire tray.

Slice and serve warm with a generous portion of Rodda's Cornish Clotted Cream, dusted with icing sugar.

*C*harlotte's Tea House

Fresh home-cooked food, speciality leaf teas, and peace

☎ 01872 263706
✉ teahouse@btconnect.com

Map ref 1 - SW65

Coinage Hall, 1 Boscawen Street,
TRURO, TR1 2QU
*Truro city centre, next to War
Memorial.*
Owner(s): Joan & Mike Pollard
☕ Open Mon-Sat 10am-5pm; Tea
served all day; Closed Sun; Booking
possible; Set tea price(s) from £6
(High Tea); No credit cards; Seats 60;
No smoking; No dogs

*T*his lovingly-restored Victorian tea house in the centre of busy Truro provides a peaceful sanctuary from the traffic noise. In these elegant surroundings, the tasteful menu offers an irresistible variety of toasted and plain sandwiches, omelettes, jacket potatoes and salads (to name just some of the choices). The good news is that the delicious set teas – cream teas with scones and high teas with sandwiches and home-made cakes – are served all day. You could choose to order China Yunnan, Jasmine or the Charlotte house blend with a toasted teacake, muffin or crumpet; coffee drinkers are rewarded with their own list of specialities. Try a champagne breakfast!

The Tea Guild's Award
of Excellence 2005

RECOMMENDED IN THE AREA

Truro Cathedral; Falmouth Maritime Museum; The Eden Project

---

*T*he Tea Shop

Charming tea rooms serving only home-made food

☎ 01208 813331

Map ref 1 - SW97

6 Polmorla Road, WADEBRIDGE,
PL27 7ND
*From The Platt, turn into Polmorla Rd
(pub on left, toilets on right); tea shop
half way down on right.*
Owner(s): Mrs Nicky Ryland
☕ Open Mon-Sat 10am-4pm Closed
Sun, Bank Hols, Christmas; Booking
possible; Set tea price(s) Cream Tea
£3.60; No credit cards; Seats 23;
No smoking; Dogs allowed at window
tables only

*F*resh local produce takes pride of place on the menu at this bright and cosy tea shop, and everything served here is home-made. This proud boast comes from owner Nicky Ryland, whose support of the town is amply repaid by the regular customers attracted by her delicious food. A selection of 40 teas makes her a winner with visitors to the area too, with around 30 cakes including boiled fruit cake, strawberry pavlova, and apple and almond cake always available. Ice creams are another favourite, and there are light lunches such as jacket potatoes and salads for those whose intentions are less frivolous. A highchair is available, and there is wheelchair access.

The Tea Guild's Award
of Excellence 2005

RECOMMENDED IN THE AREA

Camel Trail for walking and cycling; Coastal walks; Pencarrow House

47

Boiled Fruit Cake

Recipe supplied by The Tea Shop, Wadebridge (page 47)
An old family Cornish recipe

Ingredients

4oz (110g) margarine
6oz (175g) granulated sugar
14oz (450g) fruit (sultanas)
8 fl oz (250ml) water
1 level teaspoon bicarbonate of soda
2 level teaspoon mixed spice
4oz (110g) plain flour
4oz (110g) self-raising flour
pinch of salt
2 free-range eggs (beaten)

Method

You will need an 8in greased cake tin and a heavy-based saucepan. Pre-heat the oven to gas mark 4/350°F/180°C.

Put all ingredients except flours, salt and eggs into the saucepan, and bring to the boil. Boil for one minute, then leave to cool.

Sieve the flours and salt into a bowl and add the eggs. Add the cooled fruit mix and blend well with a wooden spoon. Transfer to the tin and bake for 1–1¼ hours on top shelf of oven.

Test with a skewer. Leave to cool in tin for 10–15 minutes and turn out onto a wire rack.

Cumbria

Cumbria is a county rich in traditional recipes. Well-known foods include Cumberland sausage, a long, thin sausage usually presented coiled on the plate, and Cumberland sauce, made with thickened redcurrant jelly, port and citrus fruit, and served with ham, venison and lamb.

Cumberland rum butter, a hard sauce of butter, brown sugar and rum, is at the heart of a charming old custom. Visitors to see a newborn baby were given rum butter and oatcakes to eat and in turn would leave a silver coin. On the day of the christening, when the butter bowl had been emptied, it would be used to hold the coins. A bowl with plenty of buttery coins sticking to it would augur well for the baby's future prosperity.

Kendal mint cake (much more of a sweet than a cake) has been made in the town since 1869, and famously sustained Sir Edmund Hillary and Tensing Norgay during their successful assault on Mount Everest in 1953. Legend has it that they stopped for a nibble at the summit. Mint cake remains an indispensable addition to the fell walker's rations – light to carry and packed with energy. Grasmere gingerbread is another old favourite, much more like shortbread to eat than any other kind of ginger cake (or bread). Like Kendal mint cake, it is still made and sold locally.

Armathwaite Hall ★★★★ ◉

A stately home set in 400 acres with exceptional views of Bassenthwaite Lake and the bulky outline of Skiddaw

☎ 017687 76551
📠 017687 76220
📧 reservations@
   armathwaite-hall.com
🌐 www.armathwaite-hall.com

Map ref 5 - NY23

BASSENTHWAITE, CA12 4RE
M6 to Penrith, junct 40, A66 to Keswick rdbt, A591 signed Carlisle. 8 miles to Castle Inn junct, left, hotel 300 yds ahead.
☕ Open daily; Tea served 2pm-5pm; Booking possible; Set tea price(s) Full Afternoon Tea £13.95; Seats 80; Smoking in Hall Lounge only; No dogs; Parking 100
🛏 43 Rooms

*I*nviting public rooms with roaring log fires, fine art and antique pieces are just part of the appeal of this impressive stone-built, 17th-century mansion. The hotel enjoys a stunning location on Bassenthwaite Lake, surrounded by its own extensive deer park and woodland, amid Lakeland fells in an area beloved of William Wordsworth. Country house traditions are proudly upheld at Armathwaite Hall, and not least among them is the splendid afternoon tea served in the Lake View Lounge or Hall Lounge. The full meal comprises a selection of sandwiches, scones, jam and cream, cakes and biscuits – all home-made. There is a good choice of sandwiches, toasties or panini rolls, though guests can simply opt for strawberries and cream, or a fresh cream meringue or éclair. This is a popular treat so booking is advisable on bank holiday weekends. The Hall offers full hotel facilities, including the Spa Leisure Club and outdoor pursuits. No dogs.

RECOMMENDED IN THE AREA

Wordsworth House; Cars of the Stars; Trotters World of Animals

Hazelmere Café and Bakery

A tea-lover's heaven, with delicious food to match

☎ 015395 32972
📠 015395 34101
✉ hazelmeregrange@yahoo.co.uk

Map ref 5 - SD37

1 Yewbarrow Terrace,
GRANGE-OVER-SANDS, LA11 6ED
*From A590 take B5277 into
Grange-over-Sands. Pass the station, then
1st left at mini-rdbt. Hazelmere is 1st two
properties on right.*
Owner(s): Dorothy & Ian Stubley
Open Winter: 10am-4.30pm; summer:
10am-5pm; Tea served all day; Closed 25-26
Dec, 1 Jan; Booking possible; Set tea price(s)
Hazelmere Afternoon Tea (served 2pm-4pm)
£6.95; Cumbrian Cream Tea £3.25; Seats 80
+ 8 outside; No smoking

*E*xpect at least 28 different types of tea from all around the world at this award-winning tea shop. Praise has been heaped on it for the variety and quality of its 'cuppas', as well as the range of freshly-made and locally-sourced meals and snacks that are served here. Bread, cakes, chutneys, pâtés and preserves are all baked on the premises, and offered alongside local pheasant burger, Cumbria lamb tattie pot, and Stalker's casserole. Tea time specialities include Cumberland Rum Nicky, vanilla slices, and scones made with apricot and yoghurt, and the large gracious tea room with its open fire or summer verandah can be found in a handsome Victorian arcade.

The Tea Guild's Award
of Excellence 2005

RECOMMENDED IN THE AREA
Priory Gatehouse, Cartmel (NT); Lakeside & Haverthwaite Railway

Damson Cheese

Recipe supplied by Hazelmere Café and Bakery
(page 51)

Serves 8

Ingredients

4lb/2kg damsons, washed and all stalks and leaves removed
1/2 pint /275ml water
Preserving sugar
1 teaspoon mixed spice

Method

Cook damsons in water until soft.
Push cooked damsons while still warm through a sieve, retrieving as
much pulp as possible.
Measure the pulp and allow 12oz/350g/sugar to every 1 pint/570ml.
Put the pulp and sugar into a pan, and stir constantly till sugar has
dissolved.
Add mixed spice and simmer until thick, stirring frequently.
Once damson cheese is very thick, pot into clean jars and seal
immediately.

Note:

It was traditional for fruit cheeses to be turned out from a mould once set
and sliced as for dairy cheese – hence the name! Therefore, alternatively
the hot mixture can be potted into small containers such as ramekins,
which have been greased with glycerine; once the mixture is cold it can be
turned out and presented at the table for slicing.

Wordsworth Hotel ★★★★ ◎◎
A stone-built Victorian property in a lovely Lake District village

☎ 015394 35592
📠 015394 35765
✉ enquiry@
  wordsworth-grasmere.co.uk
🌐 www.grasmere-hotels.co.uk

Map ref 7 - NY30

GRASMERE, LA22 9SW
A591 from Windermere, then B5287 into Grasmere.
☕ Open daily; Tea served 3.30pm-5.15pm; Booking possible; Set tea price(s) £9.50; Seats 30; No dogs; Parking 60
🛏 37 Rooms

The Wordsworth is a privately owned, traditional hotel set in two acres of award-winning gardens. Public rooms re furnished with antiques and afford splendid views of the surrounding landscape that once inspired the Lakeland poet. Tea can be served in the conservatory, small lounge, or out in the garden. A set cream tea is available or an afternoon tea of cucumber and egg mayonnaise sandwiches, home-made scones with jam and whipped cream, and a selection of the hotel's own cakes. The hotel has its own pub next door, The Dove & Olive Branch, where snacks and light meals are served. Dogs are permitted in the garden, and parking is provided.

RECOMMENDED IN THE AREA
Dove Cottage and Wordsworth Museum; Rydal Mount

New Village Tea Rooms
Converted cottage with a coal fire and summer umbrellas

☎ / 📠 01539 624886

Map ref 6 - NY52

Orton, PENRITH, CA10 3RH
Owner(s): Christine Evans
☕ Open daily; Tea served 10am-5pm Apr-Oct, 10.30am-4.30pm Nov-Mar; Closed 25, 26 Dec, 1 Jan; Booking possible; Set tea price(s) £6.50; No credit cards; Seats 22 + extra outside; No smoking; Dogs allowed in garden only; Parking 5

An 18th-century building with a varied history, that has most recently been used as a cottage. The open-plan arrangement downstairs means that visitors enjoying a meal can chat to the kitchen staff, and feel really at home. In winter an open coal fire keeps the place cosy, and creates a welcome refuge for walkers; in summer the tea rooms remain cool on hot days, while sun lovers can take themselves into the pretty garden to bask. Locally-produced quality ingredients go into the home-cooked menu, with its irresistible cakes, desserts, sandwiches and hot lunches, plus a choice of interesting teas.

The Tea Guild's Award of Excellence 2005

RECOMMENDED IN THE AREA
Wetheriggs Country Pottery; Dalemain; Brougham Castle

*L*akeside Hotel ★★★★ ◉◀

A relaxing lakeside conservatory serving an interesting range of hot and cold snacks and a choice of afternoon teas

☎ 015395 30001
📠 015395 31699
✉ sales@lakesidehotel.co.uk
🌐 www.lakesidehotel.co.uk

Map ref 5 - SD38

Lakeside, NEWBY BRIDGE, LA12 8AT
M6 junct 35, join A590 to Barrow, follow signs for Newby Bridge. Right over bridge, hotel 1m on right – or follow Lakeside Steamers signs from junct 36.
☕ Open daily; Tea served daily; Booking recommended; Set tea price(s) Afternoon Tea £22.50 for two people; No smoking; Parking 200
🛏 80 Rooms

A conservatory looking out across landscaped gardens to Lake Windermere beyond makes a charming setting for afternoon tea. This impressive hotel, richly decorated and sumptuously furnished, has moved a long way from its origins as a 17th-century coaching inn offering hospitality to passing traffic. Nowadays a menu of open sandwiches (Coronation chicken, grilled vegetables and mozzarella), hot dishes like pan-fried salmon, and three cheese tortellini, plus such desserts as Eton Mess and sticky toffee pudding, greet visitors looking for a light repast for lunch and throughout the afternoon. A full afternoon tea – expect a feast of sandwiches, cakes, toasted fruit bread, strawberries, scones and fresh cream – will satisfy hearty appetites, while a more modest choice of scones, crumpets or cakes with tea is also appealing. Speciality teas join a popular selection of coffees, hot chocolate and fresh orange juice, and there is also a short wine list. A luxury spa will help to work off the calories afterwards!

RECOMMENDED IN THE AREA

Windermere Lake Cruises; Lakeside & Haverthwaite Steam Railway; Aquarium of the Lakes

Cumberland Rum Nicky Tart

Recipe supplied by Lakeside Hotel (page 54)

Serves 6–8

Ingredients

1lb 10oz (750g) short crust pastry
4½ oz (125g) preserved ginger
9oz (250g) chopped dates
4 medium cooking apples, grated (recommended: Cumbrian apples such
as Forty Shilling, Carlisle Codling or Keswick Codling – if these are
unavailable, use Bramley)
5oz (150g) butter (recommended: Cream of Cumbria unsalted)
5 tablespoons rum

Method

Pre-heat oven to gas mark 4/ 350°F/180°C.
Line a buttered pie plate with half the pastry.
Cover with the dates, ginger and grated apple.
Beat together butter, sugar and rum and pour
over the filling.
Cover with the remaining pastry, in a lattice topping.
Bake for 10–15 minutes, then turn heat down
to gas mark 2/300°F/150°C and bake for
approximately 30 minutes or until golden.
Allow to cool, and serve with cream.

The ports of Whitehaven, Workington and
Maryport in West Cumbria were at the centre of the
UK rum trade, importing rum, molasses and
Barbados sugar from the Caribbean in the 18th
century. As a result, spices such as ginger, pepper and
nutmeg are now popular ingredients in traditional
Cumbrian cooking. Cumberland's flourishing trade
with the Far East was sustained by the export of wool
for carpet-making from Workington and Maryport,
in exchange for spices.
Combining rum, dried fruit and sugar with
Cumbrian varieties of apple results in a scrumptious
Rum Nicky.

Derbyshire

Derbyshire's best-known speciality is probably the Bakewell tart, known and appreciated across the world, though locals would remind you of its original and proper title, the Bakewell pudding. The first Bakewell pudding, dating from about 1860, was actually a culinary accident. A visiting nobleman to one of the town's coaching inns (now the Rutland Arms) ordered a strawberry tart. The inn's hapless cook accidentally poured the egg mixture over the jam, but the result was so pleasing that she was urged to keep producing the puddings in this way. The Bakewell pudding is just as popular in Bakewell today, but the original recipe is still a closely guarded secret.

Derbyshire is also a successful cheese-making county. The Derby cheese always rather suffered from its similarity to the more popular Cheddar, but during the 17th century the addition of chopped sage leaves to the curd (for its perceived health-giving properties) created the distinctive sage Derby. The cheese has subsequently been presented in various ways, with a 'sandwich filling' of sage running through the middle, or with an attractive green marbled effect, more popular these days, created by the addition of spinach juice to the sage leaves. A fine Stilton cheese is also made in Derbyshire, in the village of Hartington.

Ashbourne in Derbyshire is believed to be the birthplace of the gingerbread man, first created by a French prisoner who made his home in the town after the Napoleonic wars. His recipe has been handed down through the generations, and the gingerbread men are still proudly made today.

Northern Tea Merchants

Excellent teas to sample with the traditional afternoon accompaniments, or to buy from a wide specialist range

T 01246 232600
F 01246 555991
E enquiries@northern-tea.com
W www.northern-tea.com

Map ref 8 - SK37

Crown House, 193 Chatsworth Road, Brampton, CHESTERFIELD, S40 2BA
M1 junct 29, A617 Chesterfield; from rdbt at end of A617, follow signs for A619 Baslow. At rdbt at end of short dual carriageway take 2nd exit between B&Q and Wickes, to Chatsworth Rd. Tea shop on right.
Owner(s): David Pogson
🍵 Open Mon-Sat 9am-5pm; Tea served all day; Closed Sun, 25 Dec, 1 Jan, Easter Mon; Booking possible; Set tea price(s) Afternoon Tea £5.95; Seats 25; No smoking; Guide dogs only; Parking 15

This tea and coffee tasting bar is owned and run by a company of tea merchants – it doesn't get much more specialist than this! A family firm of tea blenders and tea bag manufacturers, which supplies stately homes and restaurants with their favourite brew, offers casual visitors the chance to sample the same high quality. From Formosa Oolong and Ceylon Orange Pekoe to Russian Caravan and a range of flavoured teas, each one is clearly described, and served on its own or with a additional afternoon accompaniment like cucumber sandwiches, home-made cake, or scone with jam and cream. The less exotic teas and a choice of five house blends are also listed, along with a mouth-watering array of pure Arabica coffee beans. Light meals and snacks, such as filled jacket potatoes, ploughman's lunch, salads and sandwiches are served throughout the day. Tours of the premises and tea tastings can be arranged, and there's a shop selling tea caddies, teapots and of course tea!

The Tea Guild's Award of Excellence 2005

RECOMMENDED IN THE AREA
Crooked Spire of St Mary & All Saints Church; the Peak District National Park; Chatsworth House

Devon

Devon is renowned for the quality and abundance of its locally produced food: fresh fish and seafood from its coastal waters and a wide range of produce from its lush farmlands, including some notable organic suppliers. Devon's dairy produce is legendary: rich, creamy milk crafted into fine farmhouse cheeses, butter, ice creams, yoghurts and thick, golden clotted cream.

The Devon cream tea is a grand tradition, widely enjoyed in tea rooms across the county, featuring scones, butter, jam and clotted cream. Cream also makes its appearance in the Devon split, a yeasted bun, split and filled with jam and cream. Clotted cream is also the magic ingredient in Devon flats, a mixture of flour, sugar and clotted cream creating something between a scone and a biscuit. Another local speciality is Devon apple cake, a fruity, spicy, buttery mixture with a lovely crumble topping.

Farmers' markets are flourishing and are a regular feature of the county's towns, large or small. They are a great place to get a taste of locally produced and hand made foods, including cakes, breads, preserves and pickles. Local cheeses to look out for are Beenleigh Blue, Devon Garland (garlanded with oregano and spring onion), and the Sharpham range. Devon is also an excellent honey-producing area, so don't miss out on the sticky stuff.

Northcote Manor ★★★ ◉◉

An 18th-century manor house in a lovely North Devon location

☎ 01769 560501
📠 01769 560770
✉ rest@northcotemanor.co.uk
🌐 www.northcotemanor.co.uk

Map ref 2 - SS61

BURRINGTON, EX37 9LZ
🍴 Open daily; Tea served 2.30pm-
5pm; Closed when guests reserve
'exclusive use'; Booking advisable at
weekends; Set tea price(s) £5.75,
£10.50; No smoking; Parking 30
🛏 11 Rooms; S £100-£170,
D £150-£250

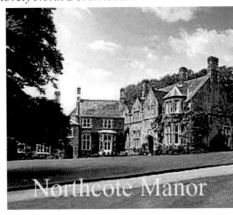

Northcote Manor

Set at the end of a winding, wooded driveway is this stone-built country house, dating from 1716. It is surrounded by 20 acres of mature gardens, lawns and woodlands and affords wonderful and dramatic views over the Taw Valley. You can take your tea by an open log fire in the hotel lounge or Oak Room or enjoy fine weather on the sun terrace overlooking the water garden. The menu offers delicious lunches as well as traditional cream teas with lashings of clotted cream. Full afternoon teas including sandwiches and a selection of home made cakes and biscuits are also available for those with a healthy appetite! Booking is advisable. Dogs permitted.

RECOMMENDED IN THE AREA

Exmoor National Park; RHS Rosemoor; National Trust houses & grounds

Boats at Clovelly

Berry Jam

Recipe supplied by Northcote Manor (page 59)

Ingredients

1lb (450g) fresh assorted berries
12oz (350g) caster sugar
1 cinnamon stick
1 vanilla pod
1/2 pint (275ml) water

Method

Place all ingredients into a pan, making sure that you have slit the vanilla pod down the middle so that the seeds come out.

Put on a low heat for about 45 minutes or until the sugar has dissolved leaving a thick berry compôte.

To test the jam to see if it is ready, put a plate into the fridge to cool. Once cooled, put a spoonful of jam onto the plate, and put it back into the fridge; if the jam has set and does not move, it is ready to enjoy.

This jam goes especially well with home-made scones or fresh bread.

Sir George Newnes Tea Rooms

traditional cream teas and friendly service

☎ 01598 753478

Map ref 2 - SS74

14 Lee Road, LYNTON, EX35 6HW
Owner(s): Lynne Cowgill &
Christine Kuczer
☛ Open Tue-Sun 9am-5pm
(summer); Wed-Sun 10am-4pm
(winter); Closed Mon (summer) Mon &
Tue (winter); Booking possible; Set tea
price(s) £14.75; Seats 34; Tea Garden;
No smoking; Dogs at owners'
discretion

Tea, served with honey and clotted cream, is the speciality here, and a wide choice of tea is available to accompany it, including Assam Kenya, Earl Grey, Darjeeling, Lapsang Suchong, and Ceylon, as well as herbal teas. The Pixie Tea (one scone with jam or honey and clotted cream) is for those with smaller appetites.

Lynton is set in beautiful countryside in the Exmoor National Park, in an area known as 'Little Switzerland'. The Sir George Newnes Tea Rooms, named after a Victorian journalist and philanthropist who left money to the Lynton cliff railway, can be found opposite the unusual Town Hall building. Delicious cakes and light lunches can be enjoyed at this charming establishment, which is adorned with hanging baskets during the summer. The Ginger Cream

RECOMMENDED IN THE AREA
Valley of the Rocks; Cliff Railway; Craft Centre

Soar Mill Cove Hotel ★★★★ ◎◎

country hotel by the sea specialising in local produce

☎ 01548 561566
fax 01548 561223
✉ info@soarmillcove.co.uk
⊕ www.soarmillcove.co.uk

Map ref 2 - SX73

SALCOMBE, TQ7 3DS
3m west of Salcombe; turn off A381 at
Malborough and follow signs for Soar.
☛ Open daily; Tea served until 5pm;
Closed Jan; Set tea price(s)
Devonshire Tea £7.90; Seats 50;
No smoking; Dogs allowed in coffee
shop only; Parking 50
⊨ 22 Rooms

A single storey building making much use of local stone and natural slate, the hotel overlooks the beach and cove without impeding the glorious views in this area of outstanding natural beauty. Tea is served in the lounge, on the deck or out in the beautiful garden. There is a full snack menu, a range of sandwiches, including local crab, and a selection of cakes and biscuits. The speciality of the house, though, is the

Devonshire Cream Tea, with scones, clotted cream, home-made jam and strawberries. The hotel's own jam and cook books are available to buy, and the car park has space for 50 cars.

RECOMMENDED IN THE AREA
Soar Mill Cove; Overbecks (NT); Salcombe Harbour Tours

61

*H*otel Riviera ★★★★ ◎◎

A hospitable seaside hotel where tea is taken very seriously

☎ 01395 515201
🖷 01395 577775
✉ enquiries@hotelriviera.co.uk
🌐 www.hotelriviera.co.uk

Map ref 2 - SY18

The Esplanade, SIDMOUTH,
EX10 8AY
In centre of Esplanade.
🍵 Open daily; Tea served 3pm-
5.30pm; Booking possible; Set tea
price(s) Devon Cream Tea £7,
Strawberry Cream Tea £7.50,
Traditional Afternoon Tea £12.50;
Seats Lounge 30, patio 40; Air con;
Dogs allowed on patio only; Parking
26
🛏 26 Rooms

*T*his delightful Regency hotel overlooks the sea; old-fashioned service and modern comforts share a prominent place on the agenda. In a town once patronised by royalty, it comes as no surprise to find that taking afternoon tea in sumptuous surroundings remains a revered and celebrated practice. Between the hours of 3 and 5.30, the delicate tinkling of silver on bone china can be heard in the lounge and foyer, and on the patio in fine weather. The choice is between the Devon Cream Tea, the Strawberry Cream Tea, and the Traditional Afternoon selection, with one of six speciality tea prepared expertly to suit your mood.

RECOMMENDED IN THE AREA

Bicton Gardens; Exeter Cathedral; Crealy Adventure Park

Dartmoor National Park

*T*he Corn Dolly

A wide choice of sweet and savoury teas, with old favourites for children

☎ 01769 574245
✆ 0845 644 5087
✉ info@corndollyteashop.co.uk
🌐 www.corndollyteashop.co.uk

Map ref 2 - SS72

115a East Street, SOUTH MOLTON, EX36 3DB
Owner(s): Geoff & Kevin Venison
☕ Open Mon-Sat 9.30am-5pm, Sun 11am-5pm; Tea served all day; Closed 25 Dec-2 Jan; Booking possible; Set tea price(s) £4.75-£6.95; Seats 33; No smoking; No dogs

*T*he Corn Dolly calls itself a Real Tea Shop, and there is no doubting the serious approach to the national drink, and the quality of the product served here. This relaxed and friendly tea shop, a popular meeting place for locals and a magnet for Devon's summer visitors, provides a delicious range of meals and snacks throughout the day. For lunch there are salads, filled jacket potatoes, sandwiches and tasty things on toast. Children will enjoy the Humpty Dumpty Tea of boiled egg and soldiers plus drink, or Tigger Tea of beans on toast. For adults there's a range of tea choices, like Gamekeeper's Tea – venison, duck and pheasant pâté with toast – or perhaps the Queen's Ransom of toasted crumpets with Stilton. The Corn Dolly Tea of scones, clotted cream and jam, and the Apple Pie Tea, a hearty slice with clotted cream, are sweeter versions, but all are served with a refreshing pot of loose leaf tea from an impressive choice.

The Tea Guild's Award of Excellence 2005

RECOMMENDED IN THE AREA
RHS Rosemoor; Exmoor National Park; Minehead

*T*hurlestone Hotel ★★★★ ◉

Long-established family-run hotel overlooking National Trust coastline

☎ 01548 560382
🖷 01548 561069
✉ enquiries@thurlestone.co.uk
🌐 www.thurlestone.co.uk

Map ref 2 - 5X64

THURLESTONE, TQ7 3NN
🍽 Open daily; Tea served 3pm–
5.30pm; Set tea price(s) from £3.95;
Seats 100; No smoking; No dogs;
Parking 185

*F*or over a century guests have been welcomed to this handsome hotel, owned by the Grose family since 1896. Tea is served in the lounge, the landscaped garden or on the terrace overlooking the bay. Guests help themselves from the afternoon buffet, advising lounge staff of their choice of set teas. There are three options: the cream tea with plain or fruit scones, strawberry jam and Devonshire clotted cream; tea or ground coffee with a choice of cake; or the traditional tea with both scones and cake. There is also a range of freshly cut sandwiches including Devonshire beef, har' and Salcombe white crab meat.

RECOMMENDED IN THE AREA

Overbecks (NT); Walks on South West Coast Path; Cookworthy Museum of Rural Life, Kingsbridge

Dorset

The lush countryside of Dorset supports plenty of cattle to provide the clotted cream that is one of the essential ingredients for a West Country afternoon tea. Other dairy products include Dorset Blue Vinny, a blue-veined white cheese – 'vinny' comes from the Old English word for mould. The cheese goes well with Dorset Knobs, rusk-like biscuits that may also be served to accompany a traditional lettuce or watercress soup. Watercress has always been grown in Dorset, and is currently enjoying a revival as a health food; blueberries, equally popular for their health-giving properties, are grown here too. Hearty traditional dishes include Dorset Lamb Crumble and Long Puddle Lamb, a casserole flavoured with Worcestershire sauce – the River Puddle is also called the Piddle, as reflected in fascinating place-names such as Piddletrenthide.

The Old Market House

Stop for genteel refreshment under the gaze of a primitive giant

☎ 01300 341 680

Map ref 2 - ST60

25 Long Street, CERNE ABBAS, DT2 7JG
In the Market Square, beside the church. Follow signs to 'village centre' from the A352 Dorchester to Sherborne road.
☕ Open Thu-Tue 12pm-5pm (8pm in July & August); Tea served all day; Closed Wed Nov-Mar; Booking possible; Set tea price(s) Cream Tea £3.40; Seats 45; No smoking; No dogs

The historic village of Cerne Abbas is dominated by the mysterious Giant carved into the hillside. This restaurant and tea-room is situated in the heart of the village, on the site of the old Guildhall, and afternoon tea here makes a welcome break when exploring the splendours of Hardy's 'Wessex' on foot or by car. Everything on offer is home-made and locally sourced wherever possible; Dorset Cream Teas come with large scones, strawberry jam and clotted cream, and there's also a savoury option featuring a cheese scone, celery and an apple. Imaginative and tempting lunches and brunches are also available.

RECOMMENDED IN THE AREA

Cerne Giant; Minterne Gardens; beautiful walks (Cerne Abbas is in an Area of Outstanding Natural Beauty)

Essex

The 14th century brought a craze to Britain for the newly imported and very expensive saffron, harvested from the stigma of the crocus flower and used to flavour both sweet and savoury dishes. Growing demand inspired a whole new style of farming in Essex, where fields of crocus flowers were grown and harvested until the early 15th century, when the industry died out. The saffron era has, however, left a legacy of local recipes for saffron breads and cakes, and is still recalled in the name of the town Saffron Waldon. Essex traditionally had a variety of local breads, including Essex huffers that are still available today. These are large triangular baps made by cutting a round of dough into equal sections.

Colchester is associated with both gooseberries and oysters, while Southend lays claim to cockle cakes, delicately flavoured sweet pastries cooked in a scallop shell.

*T*ea on the Green

Village green tea shop with superb cakes and savouries

☎ 01245 226616
✆ 01245 476619
✉ mick@
   teaonthegreen.fsnet.co.uk

Map ref 4 - TL71

3 Eves Corner, DANBURY, CM3 4QF
*M25 then A12 to Colchester, A414 to
Maldon & Danbury.*
Owner(s): Mick Hellier
🍴 Open Winter: Mon-Fri 8.30am-
4pm, Sat 10am-4pm, Sun 11am-4pm;
summer: Mon-Fri 8.30am-4.30pm,
Sat 10am-5pm, Sun 11am-5pm; Tea
served all day; Closed 25-26 Dec,
1 Jan; Booking possible for lunch;
Set tea price(s) Afternoon tea £8.25;
No credit cards; Seats 30; No smoking;
Guide dogs only; Ample free parking

*T*eapots of all shapes and sizes on display
and a collection of books on tea and
coffee to peruse leave customers in no doubt
about the function of this large pink building.
Overlooking the village green on National Trust
land, it has tables outside for summer weather,
and a bright and spacious interior where fine
white bone china sits on floral tablecloths.

There is plenty to eat, from breakfast and light lunch choices
such as filled pitta bread to a broad range of tea items: hot
buttered crumpets, muffins and cinnamon toast, finger
sandwiches, scones and cakes and a choice of speciality teas.
Winner of The Tea Guild Award of Excellence 2004.

The Tea Guild's Award
of Excellence 2005

RECOMMENDED IN THE AREA
Danbury Country Park and Lakes; Blakes Wood; Maldon Estuary

*S*quires

A cosy tea and coffee shop serving delicious fresh meals

☎ 01268 741791

Map ref 4 - TQ79

11 High Street, RAYLEIGH, SS6 7EW
*From A127 take A129 into Rayleigh
High St. Squires is at very top on right.*
Owner(s): Helen & Carl Watson
🍴 Open Mon-Sat 9am-5pm; Tea
served from 2pm; Closed Sun and
Bank Hols; Set tea price(s) Afternoon
Tea £7.50 (£13.75 for two people);
No credit cards; Seats 32;
No smoking; No dogs

*P*retty as a picture from the outside, with its twin bay
windows and hanging baskets, Squires is cosy and
inviting inside. Snuggling comfortably between a
neighbouring period property and a more modern office
building at the top of the High Street, it offers a varied all-day
coffee shop menu that specialises in soups, quiches and
cakes among several other dishes. To a background of
mainly jazz, the set afternoon tea is served from a choice of

20 different loose leaf teas and a similar
number of pure Arabica coffees, along with a
variety of sandwiches, scones with cream
and jam, and fresh cakes.

RECOMMENDED IN THE AREA
*The Dutch Cottage, Crown Hill; The
Windmill, off High Street*

Gloucestershire

A popular savoury dish is Gloucester cheese and ale, a local version of Welsh rarebit, where a mixture of double Gloucester cheese, mustard and ale is softened together in the oven (in an oven-proof dish topped with foil), and served on toasted bread. The county also has its own take on the pre-Lenten pancake feast – Gloucestershire pancakes are made with suet and are more like fritters to eat. Lardy cake, also big in Wiltshire, is another regional favourite, a yeasted dough packed with sugar, fruit and lard – great for comfort eating. Locally grown apples, cooked with brown sugar, are sandwiched between shortbread rounds to make another speciality – Gloucester shortcake.

The Queen's ★★★★

Tea remains an institution at this famous Cheltenham building

☎ 0870 400 8107
🖷 01242 224145
✉ general.queens@
macdonald-hotels.co.uk
🌐 www.macdonaldhotels.co.uk

Map ref 2 - SO92

The Promenade, CHELTENHAM,
GL50 1NN
🍽 Open daily; Tea served 10am-6pm;
Closed 24-25 Dec; Set tea price(s)
£6.95, £9.95; Seats 40 + 32 in garden;
Parking 159

A landmark hotel spectacularly located at the top of Cheltenham's main promenade. Afternoon tea taken here is one of the highlights of a visit to the Regency spa town, or the surrounding Cotswold countryside. While 19th-century ladies might have taken tea in their boudoirs, the comfortable hotel lounge (and garden in summer) is deemed more suitable here. Several classic teas are offered to accompany the Cotswold Cream Tea – scones with clotted cream and jam, and fruit or Madeira cake – or the Queen's Full

Afternoon selection: various finger sandwiches, scones and cream, and cream cakes and pastries. Other full and light meals and sandwiches are served, accompanied by an extensive wine list.

RECOMMENDED IN THE AREA
*The Cotswolds including Stow-on-the-Wold; Broadway;
Bourton-on-the-Water; Cirencester*

The hamlet of Duntisbourne Leer

Buckland Manor ★★★ ❀❀❀

Grand 13th-century manor house surrounded by beautiful gardens

☎ 01386 852626
🖷 01386 853557
✉ buckland-manor-uk@
msn.com
🌐 www.bucklandmanor.com

Map ref 3 - SP03

BUCKLAND, WR12 7LY
2m S of Broadway on B4632.
🍽 Open daily; Tea served Mon-Sat
2pm-5.30pm, Sun 4pm-5.30pm daily;
Set tea price(s) Cream Tea £8.35;
Seats 25; No dogs; Children over
12 welcome; Parking 30
🛏 13 Rooms; S £225-£360,
D £235-£370

*E*verything at Buckland Manor is geared towards the rest and relaxation of its guests. Spacious public areas are furnished with high quality pieces and decorated in an appropriately manorial style. Guest lounges are wonderfully comfortable, with crackling log fires in the cooler months. In summer, tea can be taken outside on the garden patio. A good choice of teas is offered, including decaffeinated and herbal alternatives, and your cuppa can be accompanied by sandwiches, home-made biscuits, fruit cake, or hot scones with Cornish clotted cream and strawberry jam. For the ultimate in luxury, you can add a glass of champagne to your order.

RECOMMENDED IN THE AREA

Hidcote Manor Garden; Snowshill Manor; Sudely Castle & Gardens

*T*he Marshmallow

Refreshment for energetic antique-shop browsers

☎ 01608 651536

Map ref 3 - SP23

High Street, MORETON-IN-MARSH,
GL56 0AT
On A429 between Stratford-upon-
Avon and Stow-on-the-Wold; tea
shop at north end of main street.
Owner(s): Valerie West
🍵 Open daily; Tea served 10am -
5pm Mon, 10am-4pm Tue, 10am-
9.30pm Wed-Sat, 10.30pm-9.30pm
Sun

*B*lending with the numerous high-quality art and antiques shops in the High Street, The Marshmallow is a popular venue for tourists and locals alike. Tuesday is a particularly busy day, when the traders' market comes to this delightful Cotswold town. The tea shop is distinguished by its attractive frontage clad in colourful Virginia creeper; behind is a stone-flagged courtyard with tables and hanging baskets, where customers can take tea in the warmer months. The cake trolley is laden with tempting specialities including chocolate mousses, roulades, millefuille gateaux and pecan Danish pastries, all made on the premises.

The Tea Guild's Award
of Excellence 2005

RECOMMENDED IN THE AREA
*Walking on Thames Path; Cotswold Water Park;
Buscot Park (NT)*

---

*L*ords of the Manor ★ ★ ★ ❀❀❀

Wonderfully welcoming 17th-century manor house

☎ 01451 820243
📠 01451 820696
✉ enquiries@lordsofthemanor.com
🌐 www.lordsofthemanor.com

Map ref 3 - SP12

UPPER SLAUGHTER, GL54 2JD
🍵 Open daily; Tea served 3pm-5.30pm
(Sun 4pm-5.30pm); Set tea price(s) Cream
Tea £5.95, Full Afternoon Tea £12.95;
Seats 50 (plus 25 outside); Parking 40
🛏 27 Rooms

*F*ormerly a rectory, this fine country house hotel stands in eight acres of gardens and parkland surrounded by Cotswold countryside. Stylish public rooms are warmed by open fires in winter, and in summer French windows open onto the terrace. Tea is served in the drawing room, library and bar, and outside too when the weather permits. The afternoon tea menu offers a cream tea, tea and shortbread biscuits, a selection of home-made cakes, and finger sandwiches with egg and cress, smoked salmon and cucumber. The full set tea includes all of the above. Parking is available for 40 cars.

RECOMMENDED IN THE AREA
*Bourton-on-the-Water; Hidcote Manor Gardens;
Stratford-upon-Avon*

Ma Rennie's Scones

Recipe supplied by Lords of the Manor (page 69)

Ingredients

1lb (450g) self raising flour (sieved)
pinch of salt
4oz (110g) butter
pinch of baking powder
4oz (110g) caster sugar
2oz (55g) sultanas (chopped)
1/2 pint (275ml) milk

Method

Preheat oven to gas mark 6/400°F/200°C.
Rub flour, salt and butter together by hand.
Add sugar and baking powder and mix together.
Add chopped sultanas and milk.
Mix, then roll out to a thickness of approx 1/2 inch (1cm).
Cut with a fluted pastry cutter, turn upside down and place
on baking tray.
Bake for 5–10 minutes or until golden.

Some of the World's Best Teas

Speciality Teas:
- take their name from the plantation on which they are grown (usually referred to as single estate or single source teas)
- come from a particular area or country
- are blended for a particular time of day or occasion
- are blends to which flower, fruit, herb or spice flavourings have been added.

Some Teas from China

Gunpowder

A green tea which is steamed and rolled into small pellets without breaking the veins or leaf surface, and then dried. When the pellets are brewed in hot water they produce a very light, refreshing, pale-coloured tea that has a slightly grassy taste. This tea should be drunk without milk.

Chun Mee

This green tea is made from delicately curved leaves which resemble Chun Mee, or 'Precious Eyebrows'. The tea takes skill and patience to process and the long, twisty pieces of leaf give a pale yellow infusion that should have a smooth, slighty plummy taste. Like most Chinese teas, this should be taken without milk.

Jasmine

Green tea mixed with jasmine flowers. The blooms are picked during the day, but stored in a cool place until they open to release their powerful fragrance at night. Sometimes the piles of flowers and tea leaves are placed next to each other so that the tea is scented by the jasmine. Ordinary grades are scented two or three times, but the very best is perfumed seven times. Sometimes the tea and flowers are layered together in tea chests. The flowers you will find in packets of jasmine tea are not the flowers used for scenting but a decorative touch.

Keemun

Anhui Province is in the northwest of East China across the basins of the Yangtze River and the Huaihe River, and from this iron and coal producing region comes this black tea, which is confusingly referred to by the Chinese as the 'King of Red Teas'. The processing is skilled, as each tight black strip is made from one entire leaf. The infusion is a clear, rich, amber colour, and the aroma and taste are sometimes delicately scented with a hint of rose or orchid. Drink without milk.

Lapsang Souchong

A large leaf black tea distinguished by its smoky aroma and flavour. The tea is withered over pine fires, then stuffed into wooden barrels, covered with a cloth and left to oxidise. Then it is rolled, pan-fried and finally spread out into bamboo baskets and left to dry over smoking pine fires. The infusion is a rich red colour and is better drunk without milk.

Yunnan

A black tea from Yunnan Province in the south west of China, where tea is thought to have originated. The tea plants that grow in this area produce fat sturdy buds and shoots, and the leaves are thick and fleshy. Yunnan teas are very similar in appearance to Assam teas, having plenty of little golden flecks amongst the black pieces of leaf. The fairly strong, slightly peppery flavour is also similar, and this is the only Chinese tea that drinks well with a little milk.

Oolong

Chinese oolongs are mostly made in Fujian Province although some other districts now also produce them. The leaves are often quite twisted and crinkly in appearance and are usually much lighter brown than Chinese black teas. When brewed in boiling water, the leaves gradually unfurl and reveal pink-red markings mixed with the greens and browns of the semi-oxidised tea. The oolongs have wonderful names such as Ti Kwan Yin (Tea of the Iron Goddess of Mercy), Wu Yi Shui Hsien (Water Sprite), Dahongpao (Scarlet Robe), and Fonghwang Tan-Chung. These different brands are not often found in Britain, and most blends are marketed simply as 'China Oolong'. Drink without milk.

Hampshire

The coming of the railways boosted sales of two crops in Hampshire that had traditionally been grown for local consumption. The first is strawberries, that began to be delivered bright and early to London on the 'Strawberry Specials' in the 1850s, and the second is watercress from the Alresford area. Hampshire is still the major supplier of watercress in the UK, a crop grown very specifically in shallow but fast moving water. Watercress is immensely popular these days, not only because its peppery leaves go down well in soup, salads and sandwiches, but because it is believed to have powerful medicinal properties. Hampshire is also a great honey-producing area with a range that includes aromatic heather honey from the New Forest. Another treat from the New Forest are fabulous wild mushrooms.

*T*ylney Hall Hotel ★★★★ ◉

A Victorian country house set in extensive parkland

☎ 01256 764881
📠 01256 768141
✉ sales@tylneyhall.com
🌐 www.tylneyhall.com

Map ref 3 - SU55

ROTHERWICK, RG27 9AZ
M3 junct 5, take A287 towards Basingstoke. Follow signs for Newnham/Rotherwick.
☕ Open daily; Tea served 3.30pm-5.30pm; Booking recommended; Set tea price(s) £6.50, £12.50; Seats 114 plus 41 outside; Guide dogs only; Parking 232
🛏 Rooms; S £140-£450, D £175-£480

*T*ylney Hall is a superb Grade II listed property with impressive public rooms. Afternoon tea and light meals are served in the Italian Lounge by the log fire in winter or out on the garden terrace in summer. The fabulous grounds – some 66 acres – feature restored water gardens originally laid out by Gertrude Jekyll. The full Tylney Hall Teas may also include Welsh rarebit and a glass of champagne (supplement applies). Otherwise the set tea comprises a selection of sandwiches, home-made pastries and scones with clotted cream and preserves. Reservations for tea are advisable for non-residents; parking available.

RECOMMENDED IN THE AREA
Winchester Cathedral; Highclere Castle; The Vyne

Montagu Arms Hotel ★★★ ◎◎

Historic hotel on the Beaulieu estate, with a character and charm that make visiting a delight

☎ 01590 612324
📠 01590 612188
✉ reservations@
    montaguarmshotel.co.uk
🌐 www.montaguarmshotel.co.uk

Map ref 3 - SU30

Palace Lane, BEAULIEU, SO42 7ZL
M27 junct 2, turn left at rdbt, follow signs for Beaulieu. Continue to Dibden Purlieu, then right at rdbt. Hotel on left.
☎ Open daily; Tea served 3pm-6pm;
Booking possible; Set tea price(s) £5.50;
Seats 30 + 45 outside 86
🛏 23 Rooms

*H*ospitality is top of the bill at this old world retreat, and its warmth extends equally to those resident in the hotel and those who stop by for refreshments. The 16th-century inn nestles in the pretty little hamlet of Beaulieu, where the National Motor Museum on the Beaulieu estate attracts many visitors. The historic shipbuilding village of Buckler's Hard is a short but pleasant walk away along the banks of the estuary, and the quaint High Street is worth a browse. On a cool day, the blazing log fires in the lounge encourage a relaxing doze on the comfortable sofas, and the conservatory with its outlook onto the terrace and gardens is another cosy spot. In both of these settings you can enjoy a traditional afternoon tea accompanied by a choice of speciality loose leaf teas like Russian Caravan. The charming staff bring finger sandwiches, loaf cakes, scones, cream tea fancies, shortbread, local jams, and strawberries. It's quintessential England at its best!

RECOMMENDED IN THE AREA

New Forest Visitor Centre, Lyndhurst; Walk to Hurst Castle; Otter & Owl Centre

*G*ilbert White's Tea Parlour
Restored home of an early ecologist

☎ 01420 511275
🖷 01420 511040
🌐 www.gilbertwhiteshouse.org.uk

Map ref 3 - SU72

The Wakes, SELBORNE, GU34 3JH
On B3006 Alton to A3 road.
☕ Open 11am-4.30pm daily; Tea served all
day; Closed 25-31 Dec; Seats 24;
No smoking; No dogs

*T*he great naturalist Gilbert White would b
familiar with much of the food served in this ve
English tea room, since much of it is made fro
authentic 18th century recipes. Homity pie, ol
fashioned seed cake and 'Rachel Manaton's Plu
Cake' all feature and are very popular with 21
century connoisseurs. An extensive range
speciality teas are freshly brewed to accompany th
delicious traditional fare. The tea parlour is furnishe
and decorated in period style, with original family
paintings on the walls.

RECOMMENDED IN THE AREA
Gilbert White's House and The Oates Museum;
Jane Austen's House, Chawton; The Watercress
Line, Alton

The Tea Guild's Award
of Excellence 2005

---

*T*he Wessex ★★★★
Wonderful central location

☎ 0870 400 8126
🖷 01962 841503
✉ wessex@
    macdonald-hotels.co.uk
🌐 www.wessexhotel.co.uk

Map ref 3 - SU42

Paternoster Row, WINCHESTER,
SO23 9LQ
From M3 junct 9 follow signs to Bar
End. Right at lights, left at mini-rdbt
over bridge. At next rdbt straight on.
Left after Guildhall; hotel on right.
☕ Open daily; Tea served 2pm-5pm;
Booking possible; Set tea price(s)
Cream Tea £6.95, Afternoon Tea
£10.95; Seats 50; No dogs
🛏 94 Rooms

*R*ight in the heart of this historic city, The
Wessex is a great base for exploring
Winchester and the surrounding villages
and countryside. It's also ideally placed if
you need to pause in your sightseeing and
indulge in a little something. The famous
cream teas, served in the Lounge, (which
has a huge picture window framing a view of

the 900-year-old Cathedral) are a high spot of the afternoon
or treat yourself to the Traditional Full Afternoon Tea; home
made scones, preserves and clotted cream, plus a selectic
of sandwiches and cakes.

RECOMMENDED IN THE AREA
Winchester Cathedral; Winchester Great Hall; Watercress
Line (Mid Hants Railway)

Herefordshire

Herefordshire has a strong history of apple growing and cider making. The industry probably peaked around 1877 when there were 22,000 acres of apple orchards in the county, compared to a century later when there were just 6,000 acres across Herefordshire and Worcestershire combined. Nevertheless, Herefordshire is still Big Apple Country with both apples and cider figuring prominently in local recipes, such as Hereford apple dumplings and cider cake. Tourists interested in the cider-making process might like to follow the Herefordshire Cider Trail, visiting a number of cider

makers and sampling their products.
Hereford beef is another prime product, renowned for its tenderness and flavour.

*M*rs Muffins Teashop
Local produce and fine home cooking

☎ 01531 633579

Map ref 2 - SO73

1 Church Lane, LEDBURY, HR8 1DL
Owner(s): Angela Reader
☕ Open daily Mar-Oct; Tea served all day; Closed Sun Nov-Feb 24, 25 Dec, 1 Jan; Booking possible; Set tea price(s) Cream Tea £2.80; No credit cards; No smoking; No dogs

*T*hese award-winning tea rooms in the attractive Herefordshire town of Ledbury are set in an area noted for its hop-growing. Visitors enjoying this rural part of the country will relish the pretty gardens at Mrs Muffin's in the summer, while the cosy interior comes into its own at any time of year. The menu is notable for its use of local produce, such as apple juice, cheese and ice cream. Look out for the home-made soups, toasted sandwiches and jacket potatoes, and indulge yourself with some wonderful home-baked cakes, served with properly-made tea. Jams, chutneys and apple juice are also on sale, along with recipe books.

RECOMMENDED IN THE AREA
Eastnor Castle; Weston Cider; Newbridge Farm Park

Hertfordshire

Hertfordshire was the home of the malting industry from the 1700s till the 1900s, based on its abundant barley harvest. At one time the county had 44 breweries, but only one of these still remains, McMullen and Sons, which has been brewing beer in Hertford for over 170 years.

These days, Hertfordshire is a largely urban county, accommodating the spread from London. The first of Britain's planned cities were built here, Letchworth and then Welwyn Garden City. There are no well-known delicacies associated with the county, but do look out for locally made goats' cheeses, including the Hertfordshire Speckle, made in St Albans by Elizabeth and David Harris.

*M*arriott Hanbury Manor Hotel & Country Club ★★★★★ ◎◎

Tranquil Jacobean-style manor house convenient for London

☎ 01920 487722
🆗 01920 487692
🅔 guestrelations.hanburymanor@marriotthotels.co.uk
🆆 www.marriott.co.uk/stngs

Map ref 3 - TL31

WARE, SG12 0SD
M25 junct 25, A10 north for 12m, hotel on left.
☕ Open daily; Tea served 3.30pm-5.30pm;
Booking required; Set tea price(s) Cream Tea
£8.50, Full Afternoon Tea £19, Champagne
Tea £25; Seats 50; Guide dogs only;
Parking 200
🛏 161 Rooms

RECOMMENDED IN THE AREA
Paradise Wildlife Park; Hatfield House; Duxford Imperial War Museum

*B*uilt in 1890 and set in mature grounds and 200 acres of parkland, Hanbury Manor is an impressive hotel, well known for its championship golf course which has hosted the English Open. Enjoy afternoon tea in the Oak Hall/Library. Five set teas range from the modest (the Cake Tea, a slice of cake and a pastry) to the Champagne Tea (full range of finger sandwiches, scones with jam and clotted cream, slices of cake and pastries). All the cakes, scones and pastries are produced by the hotel's pastry chef.

Down Hall Country House Hotel ★★★★ ◎◎

Splendid country house surroundings for a classic afternoon tea, with a surprise speciality

☎ 01279 731441
✆ 01279 730416
✉ reservations@downhall.co.uk
🌐 www.downhall.co.uk

Map ref 3 - TL42

Hatfield Heath, BISHOP'S STORTFORD, CM22 7AS
M11 junct 7. A414 towards Harlow. At 4th rdbt follow B183 towards Hatfield Heath. After approx. 5 miles road bears R, signed for hotel.
☕ Open daily; Tea served 2pm-5pm; Booking required for Sundays; Set tea price(s) £14.95; Seats 30; Guide dogs only; Parking 150
🛏 99 Rooms

*A*n imposing Victorian mansion house, Down Hall is set amid 110 acres of woodland, parkland and mature landscaped gardens on the Hertfordshire/Essex border, but just a few minutes from Stansted Airport and the M11. The interior is on the grand scale with lofty ceilings, panelled walls, large fireplaces and sparkling chandeliers. Afternoon tea is served in the delightful lounge, where an open fire burns in cooler weather and guests may be entertained with music from the piano. In fine weather tea can also be taken outside on the beautiful patio area. Chocolate scones are a house speciality, and also popular are the Down Hall club sandwich, or the choice of salads: chicken, fish and Greek. The set tea includes an assortment of finger sandwiches; scones, preserve and clotted cream; rich fruit cake and cream pastries. Ample parking is provided in the grounds.

RECOMMENDED IN THE AREA

Hatfield Forest (National Trust); Gibberd Gardens; Cambridge City Centre

Chocolate Scones

Recipe supplied by Down Hall Country House Hotel
(page 77)

Ingredients

7oz (200g) self raising flour
1oz (25g) cocoa
1 teaspoon baking powder
2oz (50g) butter
1oz (25g) sugar
1oz (25g) chocolate chips
1 egg
1/4 pint (150ml) of single cream

Method

Sieve the flour, cocoa and baking powder into a bowl and rub
in the butter.
Add sugar and chocolate chips and mix together.
Beat egg and cream together and add to mix, (retaining some
to spread on top).
Mix again then roll out to 2in thick.
Cut with a scone cutter and bake at gas mark 7/425°F/220°C
for 7–10 minutes.

Kent

Kent is at the heart of the south-east England fruit growing area and is well known for its apples and cherries. Fruit pies, puddings and turnovers are clear favourites with all that wonderful produce around, but there are some recipes peculiar to the area, such as cherry bumpers (a kind of turnover). Kentish huffkins are flat oval loaves of bread with a soft crust and a deep indentation at the centre, and oast cakes are balls of dough fried in lard, traditionally taken by hop pickers out into the fields to keep them going during the day.

Kent Lent pie, also known as Kentish pudding pie, is a short pastry case filled with a mixture of butter, sugar, eggs, cream and ground rice cooked with milk.

The Spa Hotel ★★★★ ◉
charming country house in peaceful Kent countryside

☎ 01892 520331
🖷 01892 510575
✉ info@spahotel.co.uk
🖳 www.spahotel.co.uk
Map ref 4 - TQ53
Mount Ephraim, TUNBRIDGE WELLS,
TN4 8XJ
*From A21 take A26, follow signs to
A264 East Grinstead, hotel on right.*
🕑 Open daily; Tea served 3pm-5pm;
booking recommended; Set tea
price(s) £12.75; Seats 40; Air con;
No dogs; Parking 189
🛏 69 Rooms D £138

Overlooking the historic spa town of Tunbridge Wells, this lovely 18th-century house is set in fourteen acres of landscaped parkland, complete with lakes and beautiful gardens. The hotel is owned by the Goring family, who also own the Goring Hotel in London (see page 90), and pay considerable attention to upholding extremely high standards in every aspect of the hotel. The atmosphere is warm and friendly, with attentive service from the professional team of staff, combining traditional British hospitality with a more modern, relaxed approach. Children are very welcome, and if you stay at the hotel plenty of activities are available for them. Tea is served in the comfortable Victoria Lounge, and consists of freshly made sandwiches, scones and cakes, complemented by a choice of teas.

RECOMMENDED IN THE AREA
Hever Castle; Leeds Castle; Penshurst Place

Claris's

A quintessentially English tea shop with beams, inglenook, lace tablecloths, and delicious food

☎ 01580 291025
✉ info@collectablegifts.net
🌐 www.collectablegifts.net

Map ref 4 - TQ83

1-3 High Street, BIDDENDEN, TN27 8AL
M20 junct 8, B2163 south. Left onto A274 to Biddenden. From junct 9, A28 south, right onto A262 to Biddenden. From junct 5, A21 south, left onto A262 to Biddenden.
Owner(s): Brian & Janet Wingham
☕ Open Tue-Sun 10.30am-5pm; Tea served all day; Closed Mon; Set tea price(s) Cream Tea £4.25; No credit cards; Seats 24 + 16 outside; No smoking; Guide dogs only

A 15th-century weaver's cottage in one of England's most unspoilt villages is the setting for a flourishing tea room and gift shop. Collectors of such diverse objects as fine pottery and Steiff teddy bears are drawn to this Aladdin's cave of treasures, found in the half-timbered High Street of what was once the centre of the cloth trade. Behind the windows filled temptingly with Moorcroft pottery, lamps, glassware, enamels and soft toys, the tea shop itself exudes charm. The low oak beams and inglenook fireplace, and spacious tables covered in lace, are outdone in appeal only by the delicious food served here. Hu light meringues are a house speciality, but equa irresistible are the wonderful walnut bread, lem Madeira, almond slice and coffee walnut cake. Crea teas come with a rich choice of brews, and there a also soups and sandwiches, or snacks such creamed mushrooms on toast. Janet and Bri Wingham are thoughtful and welcoming hosts, a their obvious love of their tea shop is contagious.

The Tea Guild's Award of Excellence 2005

RECOMMENDED IN THE AREA
Sissinghurst Castle Gardens (National Trust); Leeds Castle; Kent & East Sussex Railway

Lincolnshire

Lincolnshire is justly proud of its local specialities, which include 'Lincoln Red' beef cattle and the highly prized Lincolnshire sausages. But more exotic meats are found here too: produce from the ostrich farm at Oslinc can be found at the many farmers' markets, along with local venison. Recipes for Lincolnshire Stuffed Chine date back to the 18th century, and the dish is still served today – cured pork stuffed with parsley and sliced across the chine, so that green stripes decorate each portion. Traditionally made cheeses include unpasteurised Lincolnshire Poacher, hand-made on the Lincolnshire Wolds, and ewes' milk cheeses from Horncastle. The 'Poacher' goes well with Lincolnshire Plum Bread, a spicy loaf filled with dried fruit (not plums.) And at Grimsby's Fish Docks, you'll find a century-old smokehouse producing smoked haddock in the time-honoured way.

Chuzzlewits

Traditional tea rooms in a listed building

☎ 01507 611171

Map ref 8 - TF38

26 Upgate, LOUTH, LN11 9ET
From Lincoln take the A46 to Market Rasen, then A631 to Louth.
Owner(s): Susan & Cyril Westerman
☕ Open Wed 10am-4.30pm, Fri 10am-4.30pm, Sat 9am-5pm; Tea served all day; Closed 25-26 Dec; Set tea price(s) Queen Victoria's Afternoon Tea £6.95; No credit cards; Seats 25; No smoking; No dogs

Sue and Cyril Westerman pride themselves on the quality of food that they serve and the courtesy and service they offer at this charming small tea shop. The building was a restaurant and confectioner's in the early 20th century, and, perhaps inspired by this, they are determined to produce their cakes and scones 'the old-fashioned way' – with quality ingredients and personal attention to detail. A choice of delicious cakes, teacakes, muffins, crumpets and toast is available all day, as well as the cream tea and traditional afternoon tea – a selection of finger sandwiches, fruit scone with whipped cream and mixed-berry preserve, followed by your choice of cake.

RECOMMENDED IN THE AREA
Hubbards Hills; St James Church (highest steeple in England); Louth Museum

London

London's Chelsea buns date back to the 17th century, when they were made in prodigious quantities, many thousands a day, by Captain Bun (aka Richard Hand) at The Old Chelsea Bun House on Pimlico Road. The good captain was renowned for his eccentric business attire – a dressing gown and fez. The patronage of George III, who parked his carriage outside the shop, helped secure its phenomenal success. Though the shop was destroyed in the 19th century, the popularity of the delicious sticky buns is undiminished today. Chelsea buns are made by spreading a sheet of sweet yeast dough with dried fruit and rolling it up and cutting it into slices to form a bun in cross section.

Cockney culture in London's East End has its own traditional foods, such as oysters, fried fish (the precurser of fish and chips), pie and mash and perhaps the most unprepossessing of all delicacies – jellied eels.

It is clear from the old nursery rhyme, 'Have you seen the muffin man, the muffin man, the muffin man, have you seen the muffin man who lives in Drury Lane' that muffins were traditionally sold on the streets of London apparently up until the 1930s. These would have been English muffins, made from a yeast-raised dough cooked in flat rounds on a griddle, and still sold as tea breads today. The English muffin should not to be confused with the American muffin, generally available in the UK these days, which is more like a cup cake in appearance.

*A*thenaeum Hotel & Apartments ★★★★★ ◉

A hospitable hotel with warm, stylish reception rooms

☎ 020 7499 3464
🖷 020 7493 1860
✉ info@athenaeumhotel.com
🌐 www.athenaeumhotel.com

Map ref 3 - TQ37

116 Piccadilly, LONDON, W1J 7BJ
On Piccadilly, overlooking Green Park.
☕ Open daily; Tea served 3pm-6pm;
Booking required; Set tea price(s)
£10.50, £17, £19.50;
Seats 25; Air con
🛏 157 Rooms

The Athenaeum is one of London's leading independent five star hotels famed for offering discreet and personalised service. One of its most sought after retreats is the Windsor Lounge, a blissfully secluded room where friends can meet as if at home. Afternoons in the lounge are devoted to taking tea and a special menu presents some enticing choices. The Windsor is a straightforward yet mouth-watering affair of scones, clotted cream, preserves and traditional teas. Move up a notch for the grander Palace Tea, when sandwiches and pastries join the scones, or yet higher for a glass of champagne with the Athenaeum Royal Tea.

RECOMMENDED IN THE AREA
Buckingham Palace; Royal Academy of Arts; Kensington Gardens

---

*T*he Bentley Kempinski ★★★★★ ◉◉◉

A choice of de-luxe teas in opulent surroundings

☎ 020 7244 5555
🖷 020 7244 5566
✉ info@thebentley-hotel.com
🌐 www.thebentley-hotel.com

Map ref 3 - TQ37

27-33 Harrington Gardens, LONDON,
SW7 4JX
☕ Open daily; Tea served 3pm-6pm;
Booking preferred; Set tea price(s)
Traditional £21, Chocolate £25,
Champagne £30; Seats lounge 20,
restaurant 45; Air con
🛏 64 Rooms; S £295-£4700,
D £295-£4700

A luxury new hotel occupying a white-fronted terraced building in South Kensington, just off the busy Gloucester Road. The sumptuous interior is lined with marble, and in keeping with such grandeur, guest comfort has not been spared. A full-sized Turkish hammam, Jacuzzi baths, and a signature restaurant are among the delights waiting to be sampled. Afternoon tea is another pleasure in store for visitors to the hotel lounge, where nearly 20 teas and ten coffees can be ordered with or without cakes and pastries. For the Bentley Tea, the Chocolate Afternoon Tea, or the Champagne Tea, expect a selection of outstanding delicacies.

RECOMMENDED IN THE AREA
Science Museum, Natural History Museum, V&A; Harrods & Sloane Street; Royal Albert Hall, Earls Court, Olympia

*T*he Berners Hotel ★★★★

A traditional-style hotel in London's West End

☎ 020 7666 2000
📠 020 7666 2001
✉ berners@berners.co.uk
🌐 www.thebernershotel.co.uk

Map ref 3 - TQ37

Berners Street, LONDON, W1A 3BE
🏆 Open daily; Tea served
3pm-5.30pm; Booking required;
Set tea price(s) £11.95; Seats 40 + 25
in bar
🛏 216 Rooms

*B*erners Hotel is an elegant early 20th-century conversion of five classic town houses dating from 1835, located just off Oxford Street. The hotel's sumptuous lobby, with its elaborately carved Grade II listed ceiling, is a popular rendezvous for morning coffee and afternoon tea – the perfect retreat during a West End shopping expedition. The set afternoon tea includes a selection of freshly-cut fing sandwiches, smoked salmon and cream cheese bage delicious pastries and a home-made scone with jam a clotted cream, accompanied by your choice from a range teas or an assortment of fruit infusions. Guide dogs only.

RECOMMENDED IN THE AREA
Oxford Street; West End theatres; Covent Garden

St James' Park

The Capital ★★★★★ ❀❀❀

Enjoy a British tradition at one of London's most delightful hotels

☎ 020 7589 5171
📠 020 7225 0011
✉ reservations@capitalhotel.co.uk
🌐 www.capitalhotel.co.uk

Map ref 3 - TQ37

Basil Street, Knightsbridge, LONDON, SW3 1AT
🍽 Open daily; Tea served 3.30pm-5.30pm; Booking recommended; Set tea price(s) Afternoon Tea £15.50, Champagne Tea £26; Seats 12; Air con; Dogs at manager's discretion; Parking 15
🛏 49 Rooms

*F*rom the moment you're greeted by the uniformed doorman you'll know you're in one of Britain's smartest and most elegant hotels. The aim of The Capital's staff and management is to make you feel as though you're visiting a 'well run and much loved home', and while most of us certainly don't live anywhere that remotely resembles this wonderful place, it really is relaxed and comfortable. Afternoon tea is served in the Sitting Room, and shows the same attention to detail that you'll find everywhere in the hotel. Everything from jam and preserves to chocolate and pastries is produced in the hotel's famous restaurant, and a selection of delicate sandwiches is followed by scones and pastries, with a good choice of teas.

RECOMMENDED IN THE AREA

Harrods; Harvey Nichols; Hyde Park; Royal Albert Hall

Carlton Tower Hotel ★★★★★ ❀❀

Superior teas accompanied by a harpist

☎ 020 7235 1234
🖷 020 7235 9129
✉ contact@carltontower.com
🌐 www.carltontower.com

Map ref 3 - TQ37

Cadogan Place, LONDON, SW1X 9PY
*A4 towards Knightsbridge, turn right
onto Sloane Street. Hotel on left before
Cadogan Place.*
Manager: Francoise Barbieux
♟ Open daily; Tea served 3pm-6pm;
Booking possible; Set tea price(s) Afternoon
Tea £24 Mon-Fri, £26 weekends.
Champagne Tea £25 Mon-Fri, £31
weekends; Seats 80; Air con; No dogs;
Parking 50
🛏 220 Rooms

*I*n the glamorous Chinoiserie lounge they serve
summer drinks and exotic juices, spirits and
wines, club sandwiches and desserts, but
perhaps nothing has quite the appeal of the 'nice
cup of tea'. To the soothing sound of a harpist
playing gently in the background, devotees of the
classic afternoon repast can choose between the
Carlton Tower and the Knightsbridge, depending
on their taste for champagne and strawberries.
With or without these exotic extras, you can
expect assorted sandwiches, plain and raisin
scones served with Devonshire clotted cream and
daringly untraditional tayberry and apricot jams,
plus a selection of French pastries. Still hungry?
They serve salads and light meals till very late.

RECOMMENDED IN THE AREA
Harrods; Harvey Nichols; Buckingham Palace

The Chesterfield Mayfair ★★★★ ◉

Enjoy a satisfying tea in an atmosphere of charm and character

☎ 020 7491 2622
📠 020 7491 4793
✉ bookch@rchmail.com
🌐 www.chesterfieldmayfair.com

Map ref 3 - TQ37

35 Charles Street, Mayfair, LONDON,
W1J 5EB
*From Hyde Park Corner along
Piccadilly, left into Half Moon St.
At end left, right into Queens St,
continue to Charles St.*
Manager: Guilliaume Paquen
☕ Open daily; Tea served
3pm-5.30pm daily; Booking preferred;
Set tea price(s) Devonshire Tea
£12.95, Traditional Afternoon
Tea £19.50, Chocolate Afternoon Tea
£19.95, Champagne Afternoon Tea
£24.50; Seats 89; No smoking;
Air con; No dogs; Parking
🛏 110 Rooms

Smartly located in the heart of Mayfair, this hotel was once the home of the Earl of Chesterfield, and still retains the charm and character of a bygone era, with its wood panelling, oil paintings and leather armchairs. In these august surroundings, the more adventurous may go for the Champagne Tea, a snip at £24.50, while traditionalists will be drawn to the Devonshire Tea, or the Chesterfield.

RECOMMENDED IN THE AREA
*Royal Academy of Art; St James' Park;
Buckingham Palace and Royal Mews*

Claridge's ★★★★★ ◉◉◉

Legendary London hotel, renowned as the resort of royalty

☎ 020 7629 8860
📠 020 7499 2210
✉ info@claridges.co.uk
🌐 www.claridges.co.uk

Map ref 3 - TQ37

Brook Street, LONDON, W1K 4HR
Manager: Michiel Rap
☕ Open daily; Tea served
3pm-5.30pm; Booking required; Set
tea price(s) Afternoon Tea £27.50,
Champagne Afternoon Tea £35, Dom
Perignon Afternoon Tea £45; Seats
85; Smoking in the Foyer only; Air
con; Guide dogs only;
🛏 203 Rooms

Claridge's sets the standards by which other hotels are judged and any visit here is a proper occasion. Afternoon tea is served in the art deco foyer, beneath the fabulous Dale Chihuly silver-white light sculpture, assembled from more than 800 hand-blown glass pieces, and also in the Reading Room restaurant with its leather columns, suede walls and plush banquettes. Specialities of the house are the hotel's own tea blend (among a range of 30 from around the world), exclusive Marco Polo jelly and the super-luxurious Dom Perignon tea. Other tea-time treats include a selection of sandwiches, apple and raisin scones, French pastries and live music for guests' entertainment.

RECOMMENDED IN THE AREA
The Royal Academy; Shopping in Mayfair; Art Galleries

*C*onrad London ★★★★

Traditional tea in Riviera fashion

☎ 0207 823 3000
📠 0207 351 6525
✉ londoninfo@conradhotels.com
🌐 www.conradlondon.com

Map ref 3 - TQ37

Chelsea Harbour, LONDON, SW10 0XG
*A4 to central London, Hammersmith flyover
to Earls Court. A3 to Kings Road, right to
Putney, left onto Lots Road.*
🍴 Open daily; Tea served 3.30pm-6.00pm;
Set tea price(s) Afternoon Tea £16,
Champagne Afternoon Tea from £24; Seats
65; Air con
🛏 160 Rooms, D from £176

*S*et in the heart of Chelsea Harbour on the marina's edge, Conrad London offers traditional afternoon tea in serene luxury overlooking the water. Tea is served in Aquasia Restaurant which has floor to ceiling windows making the most of the glamorous harbour view. In warmer months you can enjoy afternoon tea al fresco on the large terrace. Afternoon tea comprises a selection of traditional sandwiches, scones and pastries and an even wider selection of Ronnefeldt teas or healing Ayurvedic teas. The Aquasia Champagne Afternoon Tea is also extremely popular where traditional tea-time fare accompanied by a glass of either brut or ros champagne.

RECOMMENDED IN THE AREA
Kings Road; Knightsbridge; Design Centre, Chelsea

---

*T*he Dorchester ★★★★★ ◉◉

A time-honoured afternoon institution in palatial surroundings

☎ 020 7629 8888
📠 020 7317 6464
✉ thepromenade@
dorchesterhotel.com
🌐 www.dorchesterhotel.com

Map ref 3 - TQ37

Park Lane, LONDON, W1A 2HJ
*On Park Lane, five minutes from Hyde
Park Corner tube.*
Manager: Marc Correal
🍴 Open daily; Tea served
2.30pm-6pm daily; Booking required;
Set tea price(s) £28.50-£38.50; Seats
100; Air con; No dogs; Parking 21
🛏 250 Rooms

*T*aking afternoon tea at The Dorchester – the phrase conjures up sumptuous images of well-mannered staff, beautifully-prepared delicacies and fragile bone china. In the Promenade you can sample finger sandwiches, scones with clotted cream and jam, and fresh pastries made by the restaurant's patissier, all served with a speciality tea such as China Oolong, Russian Caravan, or the Dorchester's own house blend (or glass of champagne for special occasions).

Winner of The Tea Guild's Top Londo Afternoon Tea Award 2002.

RECOMMENDED IN THE AREA
Hyde Park; Mayfair; Bond Street

*F*our Seasons Hotel London ★★★★★ ◉

A hospitable hotel with an exclusive address, and quality teas to match

☎ 020 7499 0888
🖷 020 7493 1895
✉ fsh.london@fourseasons.com
🌐 www.fourseasons.com

Map ref 3 - TQ37

Hamilton Place, Park Lane, LONDON,
W1A 1AZ
At Hyde Park Corner end of Park Lane –
Piccadilly Line to Hyde Park Corner.
Manager: John Stauss
☙ Open daily; Tea served 3pm-7pm daily;
Booking recommended; Set tea price(s)
Traditional Afternoon Tea £21.50,
Champagne Afternoon Tea £32.50;
Seats 60; Air con; Small dogs up to 15lb;
Parking 72
🛏 219 Rooms; S £376-£1880,
D £440-£2703

With more than 60 varieties of tea on the menu, it is hardly surprising that Four Seasons Hotel London received The Tea Council's 2003 award for Best Tea Place in London. The amazing choice, including the hotel's own Four Seasons Anniversary blend, is not the only reason for this recognition however. The elegant surroundings of the Lounge, the tinkling of a piano in the background, and the delicate china bearing sandwiches, warm scones with clotted cream and jam, plus some irresistible French pastries all contribute to an unforgettable experience. The champagne tea is an extra indulgence, and even latecomers won't miss out because servings go on until 7pm. Light meals and snacks are also available in the Lounge throughout the day, with a pre-theatre menu for early diners. This smart hotel, located in the stylish area of Park Lane, is particularly well known for its hospitality and service.

RECOMMENDED IN THE AREA
Harrods; Buckingham Palace; Hyde Park

Recipe supplied The Four Seasons Hotel London
(page 89)

Ingredients

4½oz (125g) sugar
4fl oz (100ml) egg yolk (the yolks of 5 eggs)
7fl oz (250ml) whipping cream
¾oz (20g) Earl Grey tea bags
7½oz (220g) dark chocolate
5½oz (160g) milk chocolate

Method

Beat the egg yolks and sugar till thick and white.
Boil together the cream and the tea bags.
Take the cream off the stove and strain the mixture over the chocolate. Stir until the chocolate has dissolved.
Beat the whipping cream.
Slowly mix together the chocolate and egg yolk mixtures.
Slowly mix in the beaten whipped cream.
Pour into a glass or cake, and refrigerate for 2 hours until set.

*T*he Goring ★★★★★ ◎◎

A highlight of a visit or stay – the Goring Tea

📞 020 7396 9000
📠 020 7834 4393
✉ reception@goringhotel.co.uk
🌐 www.goringhotel.co.uk

Map ref 3 - TQ37

Beeston Place, Grosvenor Gardens, LONDON, SW1W 0JW
Off Grosvenor Gardens, between Victoria Station and Buckingham Palace.
🍵 Open daily; Tea served 3.30pm-5pm; Booking possible; Set tea price(s) Traditional Goring Tea £17.50; Seats 50; No smoking area available; Air con; No dogs; Parking 8
🛏 73 Rooms

*E*ver since the Goring opened its doors in 1910, afternoon tea has been a constant feature. This icon of hospitality serves its classic set tea in the comfort of various reception rooms including the Lounge and the Terrace. The menu is long, and probably best enjoyed in the company of friends gathered for an enjoyable chat; start with a selection of sandwiches, move on to home-made scones with clotted cream and jam, then try some of the traditional pastries – don't forget to keep a little space for the Goring fruit cake, or a portion of sachertorte with Chantilly cream. Several speciality teas and the house blend will accompany this feast.

RECOMMENDED IN THE AREA
Queen's Gallery; Buckingham Palace and Royal Mews; Westminster Abbey

---

*T*he Landmark London ★★★★★ ◎

One of the last truly grand railway hotels

📞 020 7631 8000
📠 020 7631 8080
✉ reservations@thelandmark.co.uk
🌐 www.landmarklondon.co.uk

Map ref 3 - TQ37

222 Marylebone Road, LONDON, NW1 6JQ
Adjacent to Marylebone Station and near Paddington Station.
Restaurant Manager: Gerard Dallas
🍵 Open daily; Tea served 3pm-6pm; Booking recommended; Set tea price(s) £22.50, £29.50; Seats 80; Air con; No dogs; Parking 80
🛏 299 Rooms

*D*ating from 1899, when it opened as the Great Central Hotel, The Landmark combines a triumphant sense of scale and Victorian opulence with distinctive contemporary style. The Winter Garden Tea comprises assorted sandwiches, tea breads, scones, preserves and clotted cream, French pastries and freshly brewed leaf tea from a good selection. The Landmark Tea adds strawberries and cream and a glass of champagne.

RECOMMENDED IN THE AREA
Madame Tussaud's; Regents Park; The Wallace Collection

Redcurrant Bakewell Tart

Recipe supplied by The Landmark London (page 91)

Makes 1 pie (12 portions) or 45 petit fours

Ingredients

3 eggs
1½oz (40g) caster sugar
2oz (50g) ground hazelnuts (or almonds)
2oz (50g) icing sugar
¾oz (20g) plain flour
9oz (250g) redcurrants (fresh or frozen)
1 good quality bought pie case
fresh redcurrants still attached to the branch, for garnish
icing sugar for dusting
clotted cream to serve

Method

Preheat oven to gas mark 3/ 325°F/170°C. Partially bake pie case until just starting to turn golden brown.
Separate eggs and reserve the yolks for another recipe.
Whisk egg whites until thick. Add sugar and continue to whisk until at meringue stage.
Carefully fold in ground hazelnuts, icing sugar and flour. If using fresh redcurrants, add these now as well. If using frozen redcurrants, ensure that you add them straight from the freezer and do not allow them to thaw beforehand, as this will make the mix too wet.
Pour the mixture into the cooled pie case and return to the oven for approximately 30 minutes. Remove from oven and cool on a wire rack.

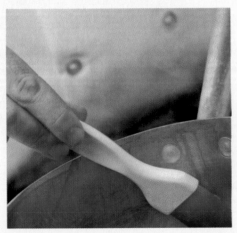

To serve:

If serving as one pie – dust with icing sugar and cut into desired number of wedges; serve with clotted cream, garnished with a small bunch of redcurrants.
If serving as petits fours – dust with icing sugar and garnish with a single redcurrant per piece.

The Lanesborough ★★★★ ◉◉

ward winning teas in splendid surroundings

☎ 020 7259 5599
🖷 020 7259 5606
📧 info@lanesborough.co.uk
🌐 www.lanesborough.com

Map ref 3 - TQ37

Hyde Park Corner, LONDON,
SW1X 7TA
Situated at Hyde Park Corner.
Manager: Karl Kessab
🍵 Open daily; Tea served 3.30pm-
6pm (4pm Sun); Closed 25 Dec;
Booking required; Set tea price(s) £28,
£37; Seats 120; Air con; Parking 38
🛏 95 Rooms

A conservatory restaurant with a glass roof reminiscent of the Brighton Pavilion is the atmospheric venue for a [cl]assic English afternoon event. The Chinoiserie theme, [e]mphasised by large potted palms and delicate flower [ar]rangements, creates a bright and welcoming setting at tea [ti]me. While a pianist plays in the background, guests can [en]joy a generous selection of delicate sandwiches, followed [by] home made pastries and cakes, and freshly baked [sc]ones with clotted cream and home made strawberry jam.

For a real occasion enjoy the 'Belgravia Tea' and have a glass of champagne and strawberries.

The Tea Guild's
Top London
Tea Place 2005

RECOMMENDED IN THE AREA
Buckingham Palace; Knightsbridge shops;Royal Academy

The Lowndes Hotel ★★★★

Reassuringly traditional afternoon teas in a stylish setting

☎ 020 7823 1234
🖷 020 7235 1154
📧 contact@lowndeshotel.com
🌐 www.lowndeshotel.com

Map ref 3 - TQ37

21 Lowndes Street, Knightsbridge, LONDON,
SW1X 9ES
From Brompton Rd, left into Sloane St. Left into Pont St; Lowndes St next left.
Manager: Jane Renton
🍵 Open daily; Tea served 3pm-6pm;
Booking recommended; Set tea price(s)
Traditional Afternoon Tea £16; Lowndes
High Tea £21 (includes a glass of pink
champagne); Seats 60 + 30 on terrace;
Air con; Parking
🛏 78 Rooms

RECOMMENDED IN THE AREA
Victoria and Albert Museum; Natural History Museum; Science Museum; Buckingham Palace

A boutique hotel with a very upmarket address – The Lowndes is within walking distance of [H]arrods and Harvey Nichols. After a hectic shopping [sp]ree, or a tour of the capital, the classic afternoon [te]a served in the Citronelle or lobby lounge will come [a]s a refreshing pick-me-up. For a fixed price you can indulge in finger sandwiches, fresh scones with Cornish clotted cream and preserves, a variety of cakes, and a pot of one of a dozen teas. Coffee drinkers are also generously accommodated, and there is a choice of tantalising desserts if the whole set tea package is too intimidating.

*M*andarin Oriental Hyde Park ★★★★★
An elegant hotel in the heart of Knightsbridge

☎ 020 7235 2000
🖷 020 7235 2001
✉ molon-reservations@mohg.com
🌐 www.mandarinoriental.com/london

Map ref 3 - TQ37

66 Knightsbridge, LONDON, SW1X 7LA
Harrods on right, hotel 0.5m on left opposite Harvey Nichols.
☕ Open daily; Tea served 3pm-6pm
(3.30pm-6pm at weekends); Booking
advisable at weekends; Set tea price(s) £23,
£26; Seats 100; Air con; Parking 13
🛏 200 Rooms

*O*ne of London's grandest hotels, built in 1898 Mandarin Oriental Hyde Park boasts views of both Hyde Park and Knightsbridge. Afternoon tea is served in The Park Restaurant, where every table enjoys a park view. This restaurant is also open for breakfast, lunch and dinner, with dishes from around the world. Traditional afternoon tea offers assorted finger sandwiches, freshly baked scones and tea breads with preserves, plus a choice of home-made cakes and pastries. A speciality of the house is the delicious rose petal jam. You can also order a glass of Moët & Chandon or Dom Perignon as part of a set tea. Booking advisable at weekends. No dogs.

RECOMMENDED IN THE AREA
Serpentine Gallery; Apsley House (Wellington Museum); V&A Museum

---

*L*e Meridien Piccadilly ★★★★★
A wonderful location and an atmosphere of elegance

☎ 0870 400 8400
🖷 020 7437 3574
✉ lmpiccres@lemeridien.com
🌐 www.lemeridien.com

Map ref 3 - TQ37

21 Piccadilly, LONDON, W1J 0BH
100 metres from Piccadilly Circus.
☕ Open daily; Tea served 3pm-6pm;
Booking possible; Set tea price(s)
Traditional Afternoon Tea £25,
Champagne Tea £32, Cheese Tea
£26; Seats 44; Air con; No dogs
🛏 266 Rooms

*A*t this recently refurbished five star hotel, tea is served upstairs in the stylish Terrace Restaurant, a peaceful haven in the heart of the noise and bustle of London's shopping centre. The hotel enjoys a wonderful location in Piccadilly, close to the Royal Academy and convenient for Regent Street and London's theatres. Tea here can involve the traditional beverages of tea and coffee, or be enhanced with a glass of champagne; top of the range is the £32 choice that includes smoked fish and caviar with blinis and, of course, champagne. An intriguing alternative is the Cheese Tea, featuring a selection of traditional English cheeses.

RECOMMENDED IN THE AREA
Oxford Street; Theatreland; Buckingham Palace

*T*he Milestone ★★★★★

popular small hotel in the heart of Royal London where tea is a time-noured treat

📞 020 7917 1000
📠 020 7917 1010
✉ conciergems@rchmail.com
🌐 www.milestonehotel.com

Map ref 3 - TQ37

-2 Kensington Court, LONDON, W8 5DL
4 into central London. Into Warwick Rd,
en right into Kensington High St. Hotel
00yds past Kensington tube station.
Manager: Guillaume Marly
🍵 Open daily; Tea served 3pm-6pm
ther times by arrangement); Booking
ecommended; Set tea price(s) Cream Tea
14.50, Traditional Afternoon Tea £24.50,
hampagne Afternoon Tea £33, Afternoon
eduction (for two people) £60, Little Prince
nd Princess Tea (for children under 12)
12.50; Seats 24; Air con 57
🛏 Rooms, D £300-£810

xpect to be treated like royalty at this luxurious hotel overlooking Kensington Palace and rdens – their motto is 'no request too large, no tail too small'. The Park Lounge enjoys gnificent views of the royal property, and with its aring fire on cooler days and stately home mosphere at all times, it is the perfect place in ich to enjoy afternoon tea. Come with friends for hat, or curl up on your own with a good book or wspaper, and relax as you enjoy the expert vice. Tea comes in a variety of flavours from rjeeling to chamomile, accompanied by an sortment of traditional foods; with the Cream Tea me freshly-baked scones with Devonshire clotted cream and strawberry preserve, while the Afternoon Tea includes a selection of finger sandwiches (smoked salmon on honey and sultana bread perhaps), scones and French pastries. For that added touch of luxury you can enjoy a glass of champagne while your tea brews. Other light meals and drinks are also served, and booking is recommended.

RECOMMENDED IN THE AREA
Kensington Palace; Diana Princess of Wales
Memorial Fountain; National History Museum

*M*illennium Glouceste*r*
Hotel London Kensington ★★★★
Ideally placed for hungry shoppers

☎ 020 7373 6030
🖷 020 7373 0409
✉ sales.gloucester@
   mill-cop.com
🌐 www.millenniumhotels.com/
   gloucester

Map ref 3 - TQ37

4-18 Harrington Gardens, LONDON,
SW7 4LH
🍽 Open daily; Tea served 3pm-6pm; Set
tea price(s) £10.95; Seats 40; Air con;
Assistance dogs only; Parking 110
🛏 610 Rooms

*I*f you're worn out from too much shopping or
exploring Kensington's museums (the Natural
History Museum, the Science Museum and the
V&A are all nearby) then you can head for the
tranquil atmosphere of this elegant hotel. Marble
floors, beautiful drapes and impressive flower
arrangements all add to the luxurious ambience.
Tea is served in Humphrey's Bar (named after
Humphrey, Duke of Gloucester, who was brother to
Henry V and fought with him at Agincourt). The
menu for afternoon tea consists of finger
sandwiches, French pastries, and fruit scones. You
might also want to try the house speciality, Graeme
Delicious Belgium Marquise, an extremely chocolate
confection full of cherries and pistachios. A wide range
of coffee and tea is available, or if you prefer they
make you a mug of hot chocolate with whippe
cream.

RECOMMENDED IN THE AREA
*Harrods; Victoria & Albert Museum; Science
Museum; Kensington Palace*

Millennium Bailey's Hotel London
Kensington ★★★★

modernised Victorian hotel where, happily, some things never change

☎ 020 7373 6000
📠 020 7370 3760
✉ reservations@mill-cop.com
🖥 www.millenniumhotels.com/baileys

Map ref 3 - TQ37

140 Gloucester Road, LONDON, SW7 4QH
A4, turn right at Cromwell hospital into
Knaresborough Place, follow to Courtfield
Rd, to corner of Gloucester Rd, hotel
opposite tube station.
☕ Open daily; Tea served 3pm-5pm;
Set tea price(s) £10.50, £15; Air con;
Parking 70
🛏 212 Rooms

Olive's Bar at Bailey's serves cool and contemporary cocktails, state-of-the-art sandwiches, tasty light bites and snacks from mid-morning to late. But if you turn up between 3 and 5.30pm, the chances are that you'll be heading for the afternoon tea menu. In the cosmopolitan atmosphere of Olive's, this institution is taken with reassuring seriousness. Expect a traditional tea stand bearing finger sandwiches, patisseries, scones with clotted cream and jam, and a refreshing choice of teas. Variations on the theme include the champagne afternoon tea or, for the fainthearted, a modest though delicious selection of pastries.

RECOMMENDED IN THE AREA
*Science Museum; Natural History Museum;
Kensington Gardens*

The Park Lane Hotel
Art deco elegance overlooking Green Park

☎ 020 7290 7328
📠 020 7290 7566
✉ palmcourt.parklane@
   sheraton.com
🖥 www.sheraton.com/parklane

Map ref 3 - TQ37

The Palm Court Lounge, Piccadilly,
LONDON, W1J 7BX
*On Piccadilly, opposite Green Park
and close to Hyde Park Corner.*
Manager: Stijn Oyen
☕ Open daily; Tea served 3pm-6pm;
Booking required for Pink Afternoon
Tea; Set tea price(s) Park Lane
Afternoon Tea £21, Art Deco
Afternoon Tea £28.50, Pink Afternoon
Tea £32.50; Seats 50; Air con;
No dogs; Parking 120
🛏 307 Rooms – S £260, D £260

The Park Lane Hotel is handily located, within walking distance of many of London's major attractions such as the theatre district and Knightsbridge and Bond Street for shopping. The Palm Court Lounge is one of the most wonderful settings for afternoon tea, with a stunning ceiling and an atmosphere of timeless elegance. The polished service and resident harpist just add to the ambience. Three set teas are offered, including the Art Deco Afternoon Tea which finishes with a glass of champagne, and the Pink Afternoon Tea, where finger sandwiches and a choice of scones are followed by a selection of pink French pastries from the hotel's patisserie and pink champagne. A good selection of teas is available.

RECOMMENDED IN THE AREA
*Green Park; Hyde Park; Buckingham
Palace*

*T*he Montague on the Gardens ★★★★

A Georgian-fronted hotel serving classy teas

☎ 020 7637 1001
🖷 020 7637 2516
✉ bookmt@rchmail.com
🌐 www.montaguehotel.com

Map ref 3 - TQ37

15 Montague Street, Bloomsbury,
LONDON, WC1B 5BJ
*Off Russell Square, close to Holborn and
Covent Garden.*
Manager: Paco Ragel
🍵 Open daily; Tea served 3pm-6pm;
Booking possible; Set tea price(s)
Traditional Afternoon Tea £14.50, Cream Tea
£12.50, Champagne High Tea £21.50; Seats
10; No smoking
🛏 99 Rooms – D £150

*A*n intimate atmosphere pervades this townhouse which feels more like a country hotel than one in central London. The beautiful gardens help to foster this impression, while indoors the stylish public rooms are staffed by a dedicated and discreet team. Tea in the conservatory is not to be missed, with views onto the grounds beyond; or you can go one better in the summer, and sit on the terrace under a large sunshade. A classic afternoon selection of finger sandwiches, scones and pastries served on a silver cake stand with elegant china plates and tea cups is a reminder of past grandeurs.

RECOMMENDED IN THE AREA
British Museum; Covent Garden; Dickens House

Chocolate Chip Scones

Recipe supplied by The Montague on the Gardens
(page 98)

Ingredients

6½lb (3kg) self raising flour
4 tablespoons cocoa powder
1¼oz (32g) salt
14 eggs
1¾pints (1 litre) milk
1lb 2oz (500g) caster sugar
1lb 5oz (600g) chocolate chips
3lb (1¼kg) butter

Method

Rub together the butter, flour, salt and cocoa butter until a sand-like
texture is achieved.
Slowly add the eggs and milk and mix until fully blended.
Finely add the chocolate chips and mix until fully blended, then allow to
rest for 10–15 minutes in the refrigerator.
On a floured surface, roll out the dough to at least 5cm (2in) thick,
then cut with a plain scone cutter.
Line a tray with baking paper then place the scones on the tray.
Wash the tops with beaten egg, then bake at gas mark 3/ 325°F/170°C
for 20–30 minutes.

The Ritz ★★★★★ ◉◉

Quintessentially the Ritz experience, but advance planning is vital

☎ 020 7493 8181
🖷 020 7493 2687
✉ enquire@theritzlondon.com
🌐 www.theritzlondon.com

Map ref 3 - TQ37

150 Piccadilly, LONDON, W1J 9BR
Manager: Stephen Boxhall
☕ Open daily; Tea served
12.30pm, 1.30pm, 3.30pm, 5.30pm,
7.30pm; Booking required; Set tea
price(s) £34; Seats 80; No smoking;
Air con; No dogs
🛏 133 Rooms; S from £365,
D £435-£2235

*I*t's what afternoons were made for, according to London's glitzy Ritz hotel, and their invitation to tea is one that few will forget in a hurry. Smart clothes are necessary (jeans just won't do, and men should wear a jacket and tie), and so is booking up to ten weeks in advance, slightly less during the week. The spectacular Palm Court makes an elegant setting for the well-dressed diners, and serves a tea to match: finely cut sandwiches without a crust in sight, freshly-baked scones with jam and clotted cream, delicate pastries and a choice of seven varieties of tea, at a Ritz price of around £60 for two. Champagne extra. Winner of The Tea Guild's Top London Afternoon Tea Award 2004.

RECOMMENDED IN THE AREA
Royal Academy of Art; Fortnum & Mason; Burlington Arcade

The Royal Botanical Gardens at Kew

*R*oyal Garden Hotel ★★★★★ ◎◎◎

Landmark modern hotel next to Hyde Park and the Royal Gardens of Kensington Palace

☎ 020 7937 8000
🖷 020 7361 1991
✉ sales@royalgardenhotel.co.uk
🌐 www.royalgardenhotel.co.uk

Map ref 3 - TQ37

2-24 Kensington High Street, LONDON, W8 4PT
☕ Open daily; Tea served 2.30pm-5.30pm; Set tea price(s) £16.75, Champagne Afternoon Tea £22.75; Seats 34; Air con; No dogs; Parking 160
🛏 396 Rooms; S £318, D £388-£453

Renowned for its breathtaking views of the London skyline, particularly from its restaurant on the 10th floor, The Royal Garden takes its name from the neighbouring Kensington Palace Gardens. It is a comfortably modern hotel, easy on the eye, with an elegant foyer creating the perfect first impression for an afternoon tea with some cachet. The location is convenient both for Hyde Park and the smart Kensington shops, and within walking distance of the Royal Albert Hall. The Park Terrace Restaurant, Café and Bar has a wonderfully open feel, with large windows looking out onto the drive and gardens of Kensington Palace. An all-day menu offers a good variety of snacks, grills, omelettes and speciality Oriental dishes. The set-price afternoon tea comprises a selection of freshly made finger sandwiches, home-made scones with clotted cream and a choice of home-made preserves, and a range of home-made cakes and pastries. Champagne is an optional extra. Parking available beneath the hotel.

RECOMMENDED IN THE AREA

Kensington Palace; Royal Albert Hall; High Street Kensingston

*R*ubens at the Palace ★★★★ ◉

A friendly hotel where afternoons are spent rewardingly

☎ 020 7834 6600
🖷 020 7233 6037
📧 bookrb@rchmail.com
🌐 www.rubenshotel.com

Map ref 3 - TQ37

39-41 Buckingham Palace Road,
LONDON, SW1W 0PS
*5 minutes' walk from Victoria Station
opposite Royal Mews.*
Manager: Norbert Stump
☕ Open daily; Tea served 2.30pm-
5pm; Booking recommended; Set tea
price(s) Devonshire Cream Tea
£12.50, Traditional Afternoon Tea
£16.50, Original Crumpet Tea £16.50
Royal Palace High Tea £22.50;
Seats 45; Air con; No dogs
🛏 173 Rooms

*L*ocated directly opposite the mews of Buckingham Palace as its name suggests, this well-regarded hotel offers stylish comfort in a busy tourist area. Enter its portals greeted by a smart commissionaire, and head for the Palace Lounge and Bar where light meals are served during the day. Everything doesn't quite stop for tea, but you feel it would if it had to! The Full Afternoon set meal incorporates finger sandwiches, scones, pastries, fruit cake, and a pot of tea chosen from a range that includes Orange Pekoe, Lapsang Souchong, and that ubiquitous favourite, Earl Grey. The warm relaxing colours and background music ensure you will be in no hurry to leave.

RECOMMENDED IN THE AREA
*Buckingham Palace; Houses of
Parliament; Westminster Abbey*

*S*herlock Holmes Hotel ★★★★ ◉

Boutique hotel in a central London location

☎ 020 7486 6161
🖷 020 7958 5211
📧 info@sherlockholmes.com
🌐 www.sherlockholmeshotel.com

Map ref 3 - TQ37

108 Baker Street, LONDON, W1U 6LJ
Close to Baker Street tube.
☕ Open daily; Tea served 2.30-5pm;
Booking required; Set tea price(s) £12, £16;
Seats 100; Air con; Guide dogs only
🛏 119 Rooms & 7 meeting rooms

*A*totally contemporary look is achieved at this elegant hotel, with clean lines, natural colours and muted tones. It is conveniently located next to the West End shops and theatres and many other places of interest. Sherlock's Grill is open for breakfast, lunch and dinner, and afternoon tea can be taken in the lounge or Sherlock's Bar – a popular venue sited just inside the main entrance. The speciality of the house is a luxury tea including a glass of champagne along with freshly cut sandwiches, scones with preserves, cream and berries, and petits fours. The hotel also has a full multi-gym, sauna and steam room.

RECOMMENDED IN THE AREA
*Madame Tussaud's; London Zoo; West End
Theatres*

*T*he Savoy,
a Fairmont Hotel ★★★★★ ◉◉◉

☎ 020 7836 4343
📠 020 7240 6040
✉ info@the-savoy.co.uk
🌐 www.fairmont.com

Map ref 3 - TQ37

Strand, LONDON, WC2R 0EU

☕ Open daily; Tea served 2pm & 4pm weekdays, 12 noon, 2pm & 4pm weekends;
Booking recommended; Set tea price(s) £24 (£27 at weekends); No smoking; Air con; No dogs
🛏 328 Rooms

RECOMMENDED IN THE AREA
Trafalgar Square; Covent Garden; Theatreland

A benchmark for luxurious London hotels, located right in the heart of theatreland, The Savoy has a noble history dating from 1889. Tea at The Savoy is a great tradition, served in the elegant Thames Foyer to the accompaniment of music from the resident pianist. A wide choice of distinct tea blends is offered, imported by specialist suppliers from around the world, plus herbal infusions and two espresso blends of Arabica and Robusta coffee beans. The set afternoon tea includes a variety of freshly filled sandwiches, delicate French pastries, teacakes, and scones with clotted cream and strawberry preserve. For an additional treat add a glass of Laurent Perrier Brut Champagne. There are two sittings for tea Monday to Friday and three Saturday and Sunday; bookings are preferred. Theatre teas, served 5.30-7.30, are a useful innovation – a hybrid of afternoon tea and high tea, with some light hot dishes. Tea related items are available for sale in the hotel's gift shop.

Sketch ●●●●

Updated afternoon tea in Mayfair

☏ 0870 777 4488
☏ 0870 777 4400
✉ info@sketch.uk.com
🌐 www.sketch.uk.com

Map ref 3 - TQ37

9 Conduit Street, LONDON, W1S 2XG

☕ Open Mon-Sat; Tea served Mon-Fri 8am-11pm, Sat 10am-11pm; Set tea price(s) Selection available; Seats 30; No smoking; Air con

Sketch is designed to be a destination for food, art and music, and is well known for its stunning décor and fabulous menus. The Parlour serves breakfast, lunch, tea and light meals, or you can buy the incredibly dainty and delightful cakes to take away (until 11pm if you need to!). There are no set teas, but you can construct one yourself from beautiful sandwiches made with paper-thin bread and delicious fillings, and choose incredible, jewel-like cakes from a display to make a cake-lover's heart sing. Florence – shortbread pastry, rhubarb and rosemary marmalade, almond mousse and orange blossom glaze, or Cardinal – blackcurrant macaroon, blackcurrant marmalade and violet mousseline cream, give an idea of the style. There is a selection of carefully chosen teas, including Longjing Dragon Well, a green tea which has been produced for over 1,000 years.

RECOMMENDED IN THE AREA
Oxford Street; Carnaby Street; Bond Street

Sofitel St James London ★★★★★ ◎◎

thoroughbred tea taken to the resonant strains of a harp

☎ 020 7747 2222
📠 020 7747 2210
✉ H3144@accor-hotels.com
🌐 www.sofitelstjames.com

Map ref 3 - TQ37

6 Waterloo Place, LONDON, SW1Y 4AN
Corner of Pall Mall and Waterloo Place –
between Trafalgar Square and Piccadilly
Circus.
Manager: Corrine Cleret
⌚ Open daily; Tea served 2.30pm-
5.30pm; Set tea price(s) Afternoon Tea
£23.50, Champagne Tea £28.50; Seats 18;
No smoking; Air con; No dogs
⇒ 186 Rooms

© Fabrice Rambert

Afternoon tea, so the menu of the Rose Lounge informs its visitors, first became fashionable in the 1840s, 200 years after the first tea was brought to Britain from China. That it is now firmly established as a national tradition is incontestable, although few establishments include a glass of rosé champagne in their set tea as does the Sofitel Hotel (a non-alcoholic version is also available!). A harpist playing in the small lounge harks back to a more gracious era, and against this classy musical background the tea ritual itself is equally reassuring and refined.

Healthy appetites are necessary for a list that includes a selection of finger sandwiches, followed by freshly-baked warm scone and crumpets with Devonshire clotted cream and jam, then a range of English and French pastries, a choice of home-made cakes, and a pot of tea or freshly-ground coffee. A lengthy list of cocktails, martinis, champagnes, wines and other drinks, along with tasty bar snacks, means that tea can happily develop into an entire evening.

RECOMMENDED IN THE AREA
London Eye; Cabinet War Rooms; National Gallery

*S*wissôtel The Howard, London ★★★★★ ◎◎
Luxury hotel in a prime London location

☎ 020 7836 3555
🖷 020 7379 4547
✉ ask-us.london@swissotel.com
🌐 www.london.swissotel.com

Map ref 3 - TQ37

Temple Place, LONDON, WC2R 2PR
Off the Embankment.
☕ Open daily; Tea served 2.30pm-5.30pm;
Booking possible; Set tea price(s) Afternoon
Tea £15, Champagne Tea £18; Seats 40; Air
con; Guide dogs only; Parking 30
🛏 189 Rooms

RECOMMENDED IN THE AREA
Houses of Parliament; London Eye; Tower Bridge

A smart hotel set by the river, the hotel has wonderful views across London's historic skyline. Covent Garden, Theatreland and the Eurostar terminal are all within easy reach. The hotel has recently been completely refurbished throughout, giving it a contemporary but elegant new look. The Temple Afternoon Tea offers a selection of finger sandwiches, home-made scones with Devonsh clotted cream and jam, cakes and French pastries. the summer you can also sit outside in the delight garden courtyard. A good choice of teas includ Assam, Darjeeling, Lapsang Souchong, camomi peppermint, jasmine, and fruit tea. For a decade touch you can add a glass of Victor Brut Champagn

*T*he Wolseley ◎
Fine food in an impressive triple-arched building on Piccadilly

☎ 0207 7499 6996
🖷 0207 499 6888
🌐 www.thewolseley.com

Map ref 3 - TQ37

160 Piccadilly, LONDON, W1J 9EB
On Piccadilly, next to the Ritz. Nearest tube: Green Park.
☕ Open daily; Tea served 3pm-5.30pm
Mon-Fri, 3.30pm-6pm Sat & Sun; Closed 25
Dec, 1 Jan, August BH; Booking
recommended; Set tea price(s) Afternoon Tea
£16, Cream Tea £7.25; Seats 150; Air con;
Guide dogs only

B uilt in 1921, this stately Grade II listed building was commissioned by Wolseley Cars as their London showroom – hence the name. Tea is served in a variety of elegant rooms: the main dining room, the salon, reception or the bar. Admire the striking décor while you indulge in a cream tea with fruit scones and a choice of teas, or a full afternoon tea with assorted finger sandwiches and a selection of pastries. Don't forget to glance through the dessert and patisserie menus too – there are inviting delights on offer. A refreshing alternative to champagne is fresh lemonade, available by the glass or pitcher.

RECOMMENDED IN THE AREA
Royal Academy; Bond Street; Green Park

LONDON HOTELS THAT SERVE AFTERNOON TEA

These hotels have told us that they offer afternoon tea to non-residents. Remember you may have to book, so please telephone in advance to avoid disappointment.

★ ★ ★ ★ ★
Baglioni Hotel
60 Hyde Park Gate
SW7 5BB
0207 7368 5700
info@
baglionihotellondon.com

★ ★ ★ ★
Copthorne Tara Hotel LondonKensington
Scarsdale Place
W8 5SR
020 7937 7211
sales.tara@mill-cop.com

★ ★ ★ ★
Crown Moran Hotel
142-152 Cricklewood
Broadway NW2 3ED
020 8452 4175
crownres@moranhotels.com

★ ★ ★ ★ ★
Four Seasons Hotel Canary Wharf
Westferry Circus E14 8RS
020 7510 1999
res.canarywharf@
fourseasons.com

★ ★ ★ ★ ★
Grosvenor House
Park Lane W1A 3AA
020 7499 6363
grosvenor.house@
marriotthotels.com

★ ★ ★ ★ ★
Hyatt Regency The Churchill
30 Portman Square
W1A 4ZX
020 7486 5800
london.churchill@
hyattintl.com

★ ★ ★ ★ ★
InterContinental London
1 Hamilton Place
W1J 7QY
020 7409 3131
london@interconti.com

★ ★ ★ ★
Jurys Clifton-Ford Hotel
47 Welbeck Street
W1M 8DN
020 7486 6600
cliftonford@jurysdoyle.com

★ ★ ★ ★
Jurys Great Russell Street
16-22 Great Russell Street
WC1B 3NN
020 7347 1000
great_russell@jurysdoyle.com

★ ★ ★ ★
Jurys Kensington Hotel
109-113 Queensgate
SW7 5LR
020 7589 6300
Kensington@jurysdoyle.com

★ ★ ★ ★
Kensington House Hotel
15-16 Prince of Wales
Terrace W8 5PQ
020 7937 2345
sales@kenhouse.com

★ ★ ★ ★
London Bridge Hotel
8-18 London Bridge
Street SE1 9SG
020 7855 2200
sales@
london-bridge-hotel.co.uk

★ ★ ★ ★
London Marriott Hotel Marble Arch
134 George Street
W1H 5DN
020 7723 1277
salesadmin.marblearch@
marriotthotels.co.uk

★ ★ ★ ★ ★
London Marriott Hotel Park Lane
140 Park Lane W1K 7AA
020 7493 7000
mhrs.parklane@
marriotthotels.com

★ ★ ★ ★
London Marriott Kensington
Cromwell Road
SW5 0TH
020 7973 1000
kensington.marriott@
marriotthotels.co.uk

★ ★ ★ ★
Meliá White House
Regents Park
Albany Street NW1 3UP
020 7391 3000
melia.white.house@
solmelia.com

★ ★ ★ ★
Millennium Hotel LondonKnightsbridge
17 Sloane Street
SW1X 9NU
020 7235 4377
knightsbridge.reservations@
mill.cop.com

★ ★ ★ ★
Millennium Hotel London Mayfair
Grosvenor Square
W1K 2HP
020 7629 9400
sales.mayfair@mill-cop.com

★ ★ ★ ★
Montcalm-Hotel Nikko London
Great Cumberland Place
W1H 7TW
020 7402 4288
reservations@montcalm.co.uk

★ ★ ★ ★
Novotel London Euston
100-110 Euston Road
NW1 2AJ
020 7666 9000
H5309@accor.com

★ ★ ★ ★ ★
One Aldwych
One Aldwych
WC2B 4RH
020 7300 1000
reservations@onealdwych.com

★ ★ ★ ★
Park Inn Heathrow
Bath Road UB7 0DU
020 8759 6611
info.heathrow@
rezidorparkinn.com

★ ★ ★ ★
Radisson Edwardian Berkshire Hotel
350 Oxford Street W1N
0BY
020 7629 7474
resberk@radisson.com

★ ★ ★ ★
Radisson Edwardian Grafton Hotel
130 Tottenham Court
Road W1T 5AY
020 7388 4131
resgraf@radisson.com

★ ★ ★ ★ ★
Radisson Edwardian Hampshire Hotel
31 Leicester Square
WC2H 7LH
020 7839 9399
reshamp@radisson.com

★ ★ ★ ★
Radisson Edwardian Kenilworth Hotel
Great Russell Street
WC1B 3LB
020 7637 3477
reskeni@radisson.com

★ ★ ★ ★
Radisson Edwardian Marlborough Hotel
Bloomsbury Street WC1B 3QD
020 7636 5601
resmarl@radisson.com

★ ★ ★ ★
Radisson Edwardian Mountbatten Hotel
Monmouth Street
WC2H 9HD
020 7836 4300
resmoun@radisson.com

★ ★ ★ ★ ★
Renaissance Chancery Court London
252 High Holborn WC1V 7EN
020 7829 9888
sales.chancerycourt@
renaissancehotels.com

★ ★ ★ ★
Royal Lancaster Hotel
Lancaster Terrace
W2TY
020 7262 6737
book@royallancaster.com

★ ★ ★ ★
Selsdon Park Hotel & Golf Course
Addington Road
CR2 8YA
020 8657 8811
sales.selsdonpark@
principal-hotels.com

★ ★ ★ ★
Sheraton Belgravia
20 Chesham Place
SW1X 8HQ
020 7235 6040
reservations.sheraton
bel gravia@sheraton.com

★ ★ ★ ★ ★
Sheraton Park Tower
101 Knightsbridge
W1X 7RN
020 7235 8050 00412.
central.london.reservations@
sheraton.com

★ ★ ★ ★
Sheraton Skyline Hotel & Conference Centre
Bath Road UB3 5BP
020 8759 2535
res268_skyline@sheraton.com

★ ★ ★ ★
The Carlton Mitre Hotel
Hampton Court Road
KT8 9BN
020 8979 9988
mitre@carltonhotels.co.uk

★ ★ ★ ★
The Chamberlain Hotel
130-135 Minories
EC3N 1NU
020 7680 1500
thechamberlain@fullers.co.uk

★ ★ ★ ★
The Cranley Hotel
10 Bina Gardens
SW5 0LA
020 7373 0123
info@thecranley.com

★ ★ ★ ★
The Halkin Hotel
Halkin Street SW1X 7DJ
020 7333 1000
res@halkin.como.bz

★ ★ ★ ★
The Petersham
Nightingale Lane
TW10 6UZ
020 8940 7471
enq@petershamhotel.co.uk

★ ★ ★ ★
The Renaissance London Heathrow Hotel
Bath Road TW6 2AQ
020 8897 6363
lhrrenaissance@aol.com

★ ★ ★ ★
The Richmond Gate Hotel
Richmond Hill
TW10 6RP
020 8940 0061
richmondgate@
foliohotels.co.uk

★ ★ ★ ★
The Stafford
16-18 St James's Place
SW1A 1NJ
020 7493 0111
info@thestaffordhotel.co.uk

★ ★ ★ ★
The Washington Mayfair Hotel
5-7 Curzon Street W1J 5HE
020 7499 7000
sales@
washington-mayfair.co.uk

★ ★ ★ ★
The Westbury Hotel
Bond Street W1S 2YF
020 7629 7755
reservations@
westburymayfair.com

★ ★ ★ ★
West Lodge Park Hotel
Cockfosters Road
EN4 0PY
020 8216 3900
westlodgepark@
bealeshotels.co.uk

Merseyside

Traditional food in the Northwest owes much to the area's industrial heritage; what better than a Lancashire Hotpot to sustain a hard-working family? Another regional favourite that has found a home in the latest stylish recipes is black pudding. But Merseyside can also boast fine seafood and vegetarian fare; salmon has always been caught in the Dee estuary (and is increasingly repopulating the Mersey), and the delicious cheeses of Cheshire and Lancashire can be sampled at their best on home ground. Local people traditionally fished for shrimps and prawns from the beach at Formby, and the famous potted version is still produced. Formby asparagus is another speciality enjoying a revival; grown on the Sefton coast for generations, it was once served to cruise passengers on Cunard liners.

*L*iverpool Marriott Hotel South ★★★★

Unique Art Deco hotel

☎ 0151 494 5000
🖶 0151 494 5053
✉ liverpool.south@
marriotthotels.co.uk
🌐 www.marriott.co.uk/lplms

Map ref 5 - SJ39

Speke Aerodrome, LIVERPOOL,
L24 8QD
M62 junct 6, take Knowsley
Expressway towards Speke. At end of
Expressway, right onto A561 towards
Liverpool. Continue for approx 4
miles, hotel on left just after Estuary
Commerce Park.
🍽 Open daily; Tea served 3pm-5pm;
Booking possible; Seats Bar 41,
Lounge 31; Air con; Guide dogs only;
Parking 200
🛏 164 Rooms

Although this distinctive hotel was originally the airport building for Speke aerodrome, the screaming crowds of Beatles fans who thronged here in the 0s are a distant memory. Guests will find n impressive conversion, full of character, stylish contemporary touches and wonderful Grade II listed architecture. Tea is served in the bar and lounge.

RECOMMENDED IN THE AREA
Knowsley Safari Park; Albert Dock; Beatles Story

109

Norfolk

The two foods most closely associated with Norfolk are probably turkeys and mustard, the latter grown in fields around the county town of Norwich, and both a useful addition to a sandwich. A not-to-be-missed treat when visiting the Norfolk coast, however, is the estimable Cromer crab.

Norfolk has its own take on the treacle tart, which doesn't include any breadcrumbs, but rather mixes golden syrup with eggs and cream for its characteristically creamy filling. Norfolk rusks are another regional speciality, similar to Suffolk rusks, though connoisseurs may say that the

Norfolk version is a little less rich Norfolk and Suffolk also have a regional approach to dumplings, which they make with a bread dough rather than a suet mix. The resulting dumplings are rather lighter, floating on the stew rather than sinking into it.

Congham Hall Country House Hotel ★ ★ ★ ◉◉
A Georgian manor house situated a few miles from Sandringham

☎ 01485 600250
📠 01485 601191
✉ info@conghamhallhotel.co.uk
🌐 www.conghamhallhotel.co.uk

Map ref 4 - TF72

Lynn Road, GRIMSTON, PE32 1AH
6m NE of King's Lynn on A148, right towards Grimston, hotel 2.5m on left (do not go to Congham).
☕ Open daily; Tea served 12pm-6pm; Booking required (for full afternoon tea); Set tea price(s) £3.50-£10.50; Seats 40; No smoking areas; Parking 50
🛏 14 Rooms

Congham Hall is a fine country house set in 30 acres of parkland, orchards, gardens and the famous herb garden stocked with 700 different herbs, including 50 varieties of mint. Log fires provide a warm welcome in the public rooms, and full afternoon tea is served in the lounge and bar, or out on the terrace in warmer weather. The set tea comprises cake, biscuits, scones and home-made preserves, cream cakes and seasonal fruit tartlets. A range of home-made produce and Norfolk delicacies is offered for sale: preserves, pot pourri, lavender, books, and herb plant (May-September). Dogs allowed on terrace. Parking provided

RECOMMENDED IN THE AREA
African Violet Centre; Arts Centre and Town House Museum (King's Lynn)

Northumberland

Pease pudding hot, pease pudding cold!" was the cry of pudding sellers in the streets in medieval times. A fortifying dish made from dried peas boiled until tender and then steamed in a cloth with herbs, onions, eggs and butter, it was traditionally eaten with pork or bacon. Another filling concoction is Pan Haggerty; as its name suggests, it is served directly from the frying pan, and consists of sliced potatoes and onions topped with cheese. At the seaside town of Craster, kippers are cured as they have been since the 19th century over slow oak fires; cockles are another local delicacy, especially served piping hot in soups. Pack a picnic basket with fine locally made bread and cheese, add some griddle scones or 'Singing Hinnies', and head off for a day's hiking in the Northumberland National Park – later, relax with a glass of Lindisfarne Mead.

Matfen Hall ★★★★ ❀❀

Magnificent country house hotel set amid landscaped parkland

☎ 01661 886500
🖷 01661 886055
✉ info@matfenhall.com
🌐 www.matfenhall.com

Map ref 7 - NZ07

MATFEN, NE20 0RH
Exit A69 onto B6318. After 7 miles turn right following signs for Matfen. Hotel just before village.
🍴 Open daily; Tea served 2.30pm-5pm; Booking recommended; Set tea price(s) Cream Tea £3.50, Full Afternoon Tea £8.95; Seats 32; Guide dogs only; Parking 150
🛏 53 Rooms

Built in the 1830s by Sir Edward Blackett, Matfen Hall has been transformed into a fine hotel with some of the best leisure facilities in the county, including its own 18-hole golf course. Tea is served in the Drawing Room, and in the conservatory which overlooks the 18th green. The menu offers cream tea and a full afternoon tea, the latter comprising scones with clotted cream and preserves, toasted teacakes, rich fruit cake, an assortment of sandwiches, and a pot of tea or freshly brewed coffee. Tea types are traditional 'black' tea, Earl Grey, peppermint and liquorice, sweet camomile and berry.

RECOMMENDED IN THE AREA
Hadrian's Wall; Alnwick Gardens; Wallington Hall

Sherwood Forest

Nottinghamshire

Lacemakers in Nottinghamshire, as in other parts of the country, have always celebrated St Catherine's Day, November 25, with Cattern cakes made from yeasted dough mixed with lard, sugar and caraway seeds. (St Catherine being the patron saint of lacemakers, spinners, rope makers and spinsters.)

An old favourite from the county town is Nottingham pudding. To make the dish, whole apples are cored and filled with sugar then covered with a batter pudding mixture and baked. This is a sweet version of toad in the hole, really, with apples instead of sausages.

Wheat cakes boiled in richly spiced milk is a special dish traditionally served on Christmas Eve in Nottinghamshire.

*L*ock House Tea Rooms

ndulge in a little culinary nostalgia with a range of old-fashioned choices

☎ 0115 972 2288
✉ mt@lockhousetearoom.demon.
co.uk

Map ref 8 - SK53

Trent Lock, Lock Lane, LONG EATON,
NG10 2FY
*3 miles from M1 junct 24. I mile outside
Long Eaton at junction of River Trent and
Erewash Canal.*
Owner(s): Teresa & Mark Ashby
☕ Open Wed-Fri 10am-4pm (winter),
10am-5pm (summer); Sat & Sun 10am-5pm
(winter), 10am-6pm (summer). Last orders
½ hour before closing; Tea served all day;
Closed Mon, Tue; Booking possible Wed-Fri
only; Set tea price(s) Sandwich High Tea
from £7.40; Seats 30 + 10 outside;
No smoking; No dogs

Idyllically set where the rivers Trent and Soar meet, in attractive Nottinghamshire countryside, these tea rooms specialise in good old-fashioned cooking. The house dates from 1794, and though it has been modernised over the years by successive lock keepers, there is still evidence of the blacksmith's forge and stabling for barge horses which were an early feature. A cell found beneath the house suggests that a militiaman was stationed at this busy river junction to deter would-be thieves from ransacking the laden boats. The Ashby family offer a warm welcome, and a menu to delight visitors. There's a choice of over 50 teas and a selection of speciality coffees. Choose from Cornish clotted cream teas, hot toasties, tripe and onions, jacket potatoes, and specials including rabbit pie, fresh poached salmon, and various salads, as well as the famous prawn tea. Relish the knickerbocker glory – reputedly the largest for miles around. Attached to the tea rooms is an antique and gift shop.

RECOMMENDED IN THE AREA

Donington Grand Prix Collection; Royal Crown Derby Visitor Centre; Shardlow Heritage Centre and Village

*O*llerton Watermill Tea Shop

The only working watermill in Nottinghamshire, with a delightful tea shop serving delicious wholesome food

☎ 01623 822469

Map ref 8 - SK66

Market Place, OLLERTON, Newark, NG22 9AA
20 miles north of Nottingham on A164, 12 miles west of Newark on A616. Tea shop in village centre.
Owner(s): Kate & Ellen Mettam
🍵 Open Wed-Sun 10.30am-5pm;
Tea served all day; Closed Mon, Tue except Bank Hols, mid-Dec to Feb; Set tea price(s) Cream Tea £3.75; No credit cards; Seats 34; No smoking; Guide dogs only; Village car park opposite

*T*he old millwright's workshop and watermill, built in 1713 and now fully operational, is the wonderfully atmospheric setting for this friendly tea shop. The old mill has been put to work again after the Mettam family – owners and millers since 1921 – decided to restore it and open it to the public. The teashop was an inspirational stroke of genius when it was set up to offer refreshments to mill visitors, and its popularity quickly soared. Sisters-in-law Kate and Ellen Mettam are particular about the produce that goes into their menu, and the result is home-baked cakes, quiches, salads and mouth-watering puddings; the cream tea with its three plain or fruit scones, jam, cream and strawberries is a perennial winner. The views from the window looking upstream to the waterwheel and mill race are delightful. For those who want to learn a little about the working life of the 18th-century miller this lovely spot is the perfect place.

The Tea Guild's Top Tea Place 2005

RECOMMENDED IN THE AREA

Rufford Country Park; Sherwood Forest; Newark (historic market town)

Moist Chocolate Cakes

Recipe supplied by Ollerton Watermill Tea Shop
(page 114)

Makes 2 x 7in x 11in oblong trays

Ingredients

1¼lb (505g) plain flour
1lb (450g) caster sugar
1lb (450g) soft margarine
1lb (450g) golden syrup
5oz (150g) ground almonds
3oz (85g) cocoa (sifted)
5 eggs
1 heaped teaspoon bicarbonate of soda, dissolved in ½ pint (300ml) milk

Method

Weigh out all dry ingredients into a large mixing bowl. Add the soft margarine and golden syrup, then add the eggs (lightly beaten), followed by the milk and bicarbonate of soda.

Blend ingredients together using a table top mixer or a hand mixer, then beat for two minutes until well blended; the mixture should look like pale chocolate mousse.

Divide between the two lined tins and bake on centre shelf at gas mark 2/300 °F/150°C (fan oven 130°C) for approximately one hour. Remove from oven when the tops of the cakes spring back if lightly pressed. Allow to cool in the tins for 10 minutes, then turn out onto a wire tray.

These cakes freeze well with no topping, or they may be topped with chocolate ganache made from good quality milk chocolate melted and mixed with a little softened butter to make a spreading consistency.

These cakes are best served with Darjeeling tea.

Some of the World's Best Teas

Speciality Teas:
- take their name from the plantation on which they are grown (usually referred to as single estate or single source teas)
- come from a particular area or country
- are blended for a particular time of day or occasion
- are blends to which flower, fruit, herb or spice flavourings have been added.

India, South Africa and Indonesia

Teas from India

Assam

The hot and steamy conditions of the Brahmaputra River Valley in Assam in north-east India produce black teas that give a full-bodied, rich, dark liquor that enjoys a smooth, malty flavour. Assam is an ideal breakfast tea, and is readily available in Britain, although it is harder to find the subtler single-source teas that come from named estates. Use milk to taste.

Darjeeling

Grown in the Himalayan mountains, several thousand feet above sea level, Darjeeling is known as the champagne of teas. The cold winters and hot summers give a concentrated, slightly astringent flavour that is prized all over the world. Drink without milk.

Nilgiri

The black teas from Nilgiri hills in the south of India are bright, fruity and flavoursome and are often blended with lighter teas to add strength and interest.

Teas from Kenya

You probably had some Kenyan tea this morning. Britain buys around 50% of its teas from Kenya, as the strong rich flavour and dark, coppery infusion is ideal for the blends that go into everyday teabags. Best drunk with milk, the British way.

Tea from South Africa

Zulu Tea

A black tea from Kwazulu, this is the only South African tea to be exported for international consumption. The flavour is lively and strong and is best drunk with milk.

Teas from Indonesia

Indonesian black teas are light and flavoursome. Most are sold for blending purposes as and are a major source of foreign currency for Indonesia. It is possible to buy some single estate Indonesian teas and these are very refreshing drunk without milk but perhaps with a slice of lemon.

*O*ld School Tearoom

Old school artefacts and wonderful home baking

☎ 01909 483517

Map ref 8 - SK57

Carburton, NEAR WORKSOP, S80 3BP
On B6034 Worksop to Ollerton, opposite entrance to Clumber Park.
Owner(s): Mr & Mrs Brearley
🍵 Open Tue-Sun & Bank holiday Mondays; mid-Jan to Oct 10am-4.30pm,
Oct-Dec 10am-4pm; Afternoon Tea not served between 12pm and 2pm; Closed Mon except
Bank Hols, two weeks over Christmas and New Year; Booking possible; Set tea price(s)
£3.25-£7.25; No credit cards; Seats 40 + 16 outside; No smoking; Dogs allowed outside only;
Parking 15-20

RECOMMENDED IN THE AREA
Clumber Park; Sherwood Forest; Dukeries Garden Centre

This peaceful country tea room is housed in a converted 1930s school, where many original features have been used to delightful effect. The menu is written on an old blackboard and easel, and the original hand basins have been kept in the washrooms. Where once reference books and stacks of homework sat on the school shelves, displays of local woodwork, prints and greetings cards are now on sale. Home-baked fruit pies, cakes and scones feature on the interesting menu, and the savoury tea (cheese scones with cheese, celery and chutney) makes a tasty alternative to the set cream tea.

Oxfordshire

Banbury cakes, puff pastry ovals filled with a fruity mixture are similar to Eccles cakes and Chorley cakes, though some versions of the recipe call for the addition of rum. They have been made for centuries and at one time they were sold on the street from special lidded baskets. Some say the cakes date back to pagan times and are associated with May Day celebrations.

Oxford marmalade has a distinctively dark amber colouring. It is thickly cut and the flavour is a little more bitter than that of other marmalades.

Oxford sausages are packed with pork, veal, suet, lemon and herbs and are generally made without a skin.

View from Carfax Tower

*O*ld Parsonage Hotel ★★★★

or guests at this smart and welcoming hotel afternoon tea is a definite priority

☎ 01865 310210
🖷 01865 311262
✉ info@oldparsonage-hotel.co.uk
🖳 www.oxford-hotels-
   restaurants.co.uk/op.html

Map ref 3 - SP50

Banbury Road, OXFORD, OX2 6NN
5 minutes' walk from city centre on Banbury
Road, next to St Giles Church.
Open daily; Tea served Mon-Fri
2pm-5pm, Sat & Sun 3.30pm-5pm; Booking
recommended at weekends; Set tea price(s)
Light Tea £6.50, Champagne Tea £19.50,
Very High Tea £13.50; Seats 60; Smoking in
bar and on terrace only; Restaurant air con;
Parking 16
⇥ 30 Rooms

This beautiful town house hotel dates in part from the 16th century, and offers comfortable eating areas for day visitors. Afternoon tea is served in the cosy club-like restaurant, or on the terrace of one of the two small garden areas on warm summer days. A special menu offers a choice of Light Tea (scones with cream and preserves, various teas including the Old Parsonage Blend, and coffees), or Very High Tea (sandwiches, home-baked cakes, and scones with cream and preserves, and tea/coffee); a Champagne Tea is also available. Other tea time offerings include toasted crumpets, home-made ice creams and sorbets, and hot chocolate or toddy to keep out the winter chill.

RECOMMENDED IN THE AREA
University Colleges; Ashmolean Museum; Pitt Rivers Museum

Shropshire

Like Herefordshire, Shropshire is an apple county. There are plenty of recipes for apple cakes, or you could try apple cobs (apples filled with honey and spices and completely encased in shortcrust pastry). Soul Cakes were made for All Soul's Day on November 2nd. Children went 'a-souling' - going from house to house chanting 'A soul-cake, a soul-cake, please, good missus, a soul-cake. One for Peter, one for Paul, and three for Him who saved us all.' The biscuit-like cakes are made with butter, sugar, eggs, flour, spices and currants, sometimes with strands of saffron as well. Welsh border tart (a meringue-topped lemon pie) and caraway soda bread are also traditional in Shropshire, as are cakes to celebrate particular times of year. The spicy 'lambing cake' kept workers going through the long cold nights when the first spring lambs were born, and 'shearing cake', a spicy rich cake with brown sugar, caraway seeds, lemon rind honey and ginger, was devoured after the shearing was finished.

*D*e Grey's

An old-fashioned bakery and tea shop serving a wide choice of pastries, cakes and speciality teas

☎ 01584 872764
Ⓦ www.degreys.co.uk

Map ref 2 - SO57

5-6 Broad Street, LUDLOW, SY8 1NG
In town centre, on Broad Street, near Buttercross Clock Tower.
Owner(s): Mrs S Underhill
☕ Open Mon-Thur 9am-5pm, Fri-Sat 9am-5.30pm, Sun 11am-5pm; Tea served all day; Booking possible; Set tea price(s) £7.60-£8.70; Seats 80; Smoking area available; Air con; Guide dogs only

Located just below the Buttercross clock tower, De Grey's is housed behind a picturesquely-beamed bakery. Inside the tea shop you can sample a thoroughly decent brew of speciality tea, or try an iced green and mandarin tea, or perhaps wild blackberry and apple. The splendid afternoon tea consists of a sandwich, fancy cake, and fruit scone with jam and cream, or you can pick your own selection from toasted teacake, pastries, scones and buns. Light and full meals are served throughout the day; the menu includes Welsh rarebit or club sandwiches, as well as home-made lasagne, salads and baked potatoes.

The Tea Guild's Award of Excellence 2005

RECOMMENDED IN THE AREA
Ludlow Castle; Stokesay Castle; St Lawrence Church

*B*ird on the Rock Tearoom

Highly-regarded tea rooms serving speciality teas and delicious food, with plenty of produce to take home

📞 01588 660631
🌐 www.birdontherock.com

Map ref 2 - SO47

Abcott, CLUNGUNFORD, SY7 0PX
9 miles NW of Ludlow on B4367 Knighton Road.
Owner(s): Douglas & Annabel Hawkes
Open Wed-Sun, 10.30am-6pm (summer), 10.30am-5pm (winter). Open Bank Holiday Mondays (closed following Weds); Tea served all day; Closed Mon & Tue; Booking recommended; Set tea price(s) from £5.50; 'Complete Jeeves' £14; Seats 28 inside, 18 outside; No smoking; No dogs inside; Parking 9 (plus roadside parking)

Some very rare teas from small selected estates are among the connoisseur's choice offered at this popular tea shop. Russian Caravan, Yunnan, several Oolongs, Lady Grey, Nilgiri, and Keemun expand the usual specialist choice, along with the house Shropshire Blend (strong old-fashioned) and Bertie's Brew (a little fruity), and visitors are encouraged to sample some unfamiliar flavours which they might otherwise never try. On the food front, one of the set afternoon teas includes a themed selection with 'something savoury followed by something sweet', and a choice of tea or other drink. The 'Complete Jeeves', on the other hand, is just as grand as it sounds: don't be surprised to see a tiered cake stand presented at your table, piled high with sandwiches, scones and cakes (booking in advance is recommended for this choice). Seasonal tea-tasting events are a regular feature here, and home-made jams and chutneys, specially packed teas, and gifts and books are all on sale. Winner of Top Tea Place 2004.

The Tea Guild's Award of Excellence 2005

RECOMMENDED IN THE AREA
Ludlow town, castle and restaurants; Ironbridge National Heritage Site; Stokesay Castle

Somerset

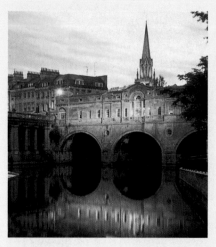

The most popular and widely consumed British cheese is unquestionably the great Cheddar from Somerset. The cheese was once made on many of the farms in the vicinity of the village of Cheddar, but today there is only one manufacturer remaining in the birthplace of the cheese, the Cheddar Gorge Cheese Company, though of course there are many other Cheddar makers in country. Visitors to the factory can see the whole process of traditional cheese making from start to finish. Cheese making in Somerset is not restricted to its native Cheddar, however, as an award winning Somerset Brie is made from local milk by Lubborn Cheese Ltd at Cricket St Thomas.

Cider-making is also very much a part of the Somerset heritage. At one time every farm would grow cider apples and have its own press producing 'scrumpy' for home consumption. These days cider making is a more commercial enterprise, though some small companies are still making cider in the traditional way. Recently the county has also seen a revival of cider-brandy making.

The city of Bath is famous for two kinds of buns, Bath Buns and Sally Lunns. The former are traditionally flavoured with caraway seeds (but these days are more likely to be filled with currants), and topped with crushed sugar. Sally Lunns are rich, light and generously proportioned brioche-type buns, which can be served with sweet or savoury accompaniments. The buns can still be enjoyed at Sally Lunn's Refreshment House & Museum in Bath. The original oven, Georgian cooking range and a collection of baking utensils are displayed in the museum.

The Royal Crescent Hotel ★★★★★ ◉◉◉

Smart surroundings for an equally graceful afternoon tea

📞 01225 823333
📠 01225 339401
📧 info@royalcrescent.co.uk
🌐 www.royalcrescent.co.uk

Map ref 2 - ST76

16 Royal Crescent, BATH, BA1 2LS
In centre of Royal Crescent, off Brock Street.
🍴 Open daily; Tea served 3.30pm-5pm;
Booking required; Set tea price(s) Cream Tea
£10.75, Traditional Afternoon Tea £16.50;
Seats 60; No smoking; Air con; Parking
available
🛏 Rooms, D £240-£850

The world-famous Royal Crescent is a striking example of Georgian architecture and a landmark at the top of the city. The magnificent sweep of buildings is the setting for this elegant hotel, where a delightful garden leads to further public rooms. The grandeur of the surroundings is matched by the glamour of afternoon tea served in the mansion drawing room, or the Dower House. The simple Cream Tea is easily outdone in scale by the Traditional Afternoon Tea – sandwiches, scones with jam and cream, cakes and pastries, Bath buns, and a choice of classy teas. For special occasions a glass of champagne makes a memorable addition.

RECOMMENDED IN THE AREA
No 1 Royal Crescent; Jane Austen Centre; Museum of Costume

Sally Lunn's

Famous tea rooms renowned for the eponymous bun

📞 01225 461634
📠 01225 447090
📧 tea@sallylunns.co.uk
🌐 www.sallylunns.co.uk

Map ref 2 - ST76

4 North Parade Passage, BATH, BA1 1NX
In centre of Bath; follow signs to Sally Lunn's/Oldest House in Bath.
Owner(s): Jonathan Overton & Julian Abraham
🍴 Open Mon-Sat 10am-10pm, Sun
11am-9pm; Tea served all day; Closed 25-26
Dec, 1 Jan; Set tea price(s) £5.68-£10.98;
Seats 90; No smoking; No dogs

The oldest house in Bath, Sally Lunn's was named after a young Huguenot refugee called Solange Luyon who arrived in Bath from France in 1680. Her native brioches soon took hold of the local imagination, and 'the rest is history'. The light and creamy Sally Lunn Bun is served by the half, topped with jam and cream for a delicious tea at any time of the day, or with savouries for a filling snack. Set in a narrow street, this is one of Bath's most enduring tourist attractions. Lunches, morning coffees and candlelit dinners are also on the menu, with a good choice of well-brewed teas.

RECOMMENDED IN THE AREA
Roman Baths; Bath Abbey; Sally Lunn's Kitchen Museum (free to patrons)

Bath and North East Somerset Lemon Curd

Recipe supplied by Sally Lunn's (page 123)

Ingredients

Peel from 3 large lemons
4fl oz (85ml) freshly squeezed lemon juice
(Number of lemons required will depend on the size – between 2 and 4)
2oz (50g) unsalted butter
7oz (200g) caster sugar
4fl oz (85ml) fresh eggs, beaten
(Again, eggs vary in size, so measure the amount – between 1 and 3 eggs)
Glass jar(s) to hold ¾ pint (350ml)

Method

Clean and sterilise your jar(s) and lid(s).
Peel lemon skin (as thinly as possible) into strips using a potato peeler.
Squeeze lemons, strain juice for pips, and then measure the juice.
Add rind to measured lemon juice in a jug.

Put all the unsalted butter in bowl over saucepan of boiling water and
melt. When melted, add sugar, lemon juice and lemon peel strips. Stir
(often but not continuously) over water bath until sugar is dissolved.

When sugar has dissolved, remove bowl from the saucepan of boiling water
and stand over another bowl / pan of cold water.
Beat eggs lightly – don't let them 'froth' – and set aside.
When the mixture is cool, add beaten eggs to lemon mixture and mix in
well.

Now pass mixture through fine nylon sieve into another bowl, which will
then fit over the saucepan. (Discard sieve contents: lemon rind and any
bits). Try and get all the juice by

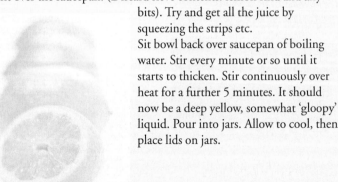

squeezing the strips etc.
Sit bowl back over saucepan of boiling
water. Stir every minute or so until it
starts to thicken. Stir continuously over
heat for a further 5 minutes. It should
now be a deep yellow, somewhat 'gloopy'
liquid. Pour into jars. Allow to cool, then
place lids on jars.

Searcy's at The Pump Room
Classical music, elegant surroundings and fine teas

☎ 01225 444477
🖷 01225 315942

Map ref 2 - ST76

Stall Street, BATH, BA1 1LZ
Owner(s): Jane Bartolotta
🏆 Open 9.30am-4.30pm daily;
July & Aug, open to 9.30pm; Tea
served 2.30pm-close; Closed 25-26
Dec; Booking possible Mon-Fri &
evenings Jul & Aug; Set tea price(s)
Traditional Pump Room Tea from
£12.25, £18.50 for two; Searcy's
Champagne Tea from £19.50 for one,
£29 for two; Seats 120 approx;
No smoking; Guide dogs only

*F*or over two centuries the great and the good have come
to drink the waters in this striking neo-classical room.
The hot spa water they came to find is still on sale here, and
many swear by its healing properties. But of more interest to
Bath's modern visitors is the mouth-watering food served
with impeccable style by Searcy's. High on the list of
favourites comes afternoon tea; a traditional platter of
smoked salmon sandwiches, freshly baked scones with
local strawberry preserve and clotted cream; also delicious
home made cakes and pastries and even a
high tea of Cheddar and Stilton crostinis. All
this and live classical music from the Pump
Room Trio.

The Tea Guild's Award
of Excellence 2005

RECOMMENDED IN THE AREA
*Roman Baths; Museum of Costume; Bath
Postal Museum*

*L*ewis's Tea Rooms

Unhurried pace in an inviting old-world setting

☎ 01398 323850

Map ref 2 - SS92

13 The High Street, DULVERTON, TA22 9HB
*M5 junct 27, A361 to Taunton. Take A396
signed to Dunster, then B3223 to Dulverton.
Tea Rooms in High St approx 200yds past
bridge.*
Owner(s): Heather Fuidge
☕ Open daily; Tea served10am-5pm;
Closed Jan; Booking possible; Set tea
price(s) Cream Tea £3.95; Seats 40;
No smoking

This instantly welcoming tea shop occupies a pair of 18th-century cottages that have been knocked into one. At either end a stone fireplace blazes in winter, and in the summer the flower-filled courtyard tempts visitors outside. Dotted around the spacious primrose-painted room are items for sale – pottery, paintings, small antiques, dried flowers and gifts – and fresh flowers brighten the tables. Rarebits are a savoury speciality here, with quiches, pâtés, and jacket potatoes, plus home-made cakes and puddings. When it comes to tea time, the speciality loose leaf teas and fat scones with strawberry jam and clotted cream prove to be winners every time.

RECOMMENDED IN THE AREA

Tarr Steps, Knightshayes Court (National Trust), Exmoor National Park

Staffordshire

taffordshire oatcakes are strongly identified with the potteries area f north Staffordshire. They are ade from a yeasty batter of oats nd flour mixed with milk and ater and fried like a pancake. atcakes are extremely versatile nd though traditionally served r breakfast with a fry up of acon and eggs, they are equally ppealing for a snack meal, used ke a wrap with the filling or ccompaniment of your choice, or s a dessert with a sweet filling. istorically, oats were the staple real grown on the county's indswept moorlands, on the inges of the Pennines, and atcakes the daily bread of ordinary folk. James Boswell sampled Staffordshire oatcakes in 1776 when he accompanied his friend Dr Samuel Johnson on a visit to Litchfield. He found them very different from the hard biscuit-like oatcake of his native Scotland. Staffordshire beef is another prime local product to look out for in the county, sometimes served beneath an oaten pastry.

Greystones 17th Century Tea Room

ome-baked food served in a relaxed tea shop

☎ 01538 398522

Map ref 7 - SJ95

Stockwell Street, LEEK, ST13 6DH
On A523 Buxton to Macclesfield Road, next to library.
Owner(s): Janet & Roger Warrilow
🍷 Open Wed, Fri & Sat; Tea served Wed 10am-3pm, Fri 10am-3pm, Sat 10am-4pm; Closed Mon, Tue, Thu, Sun occasionally closed for holidays, please telephone to check; No credit cards; Seats 24; No smoking; No dogs

reystones is a Grade II listed building with mullioned windows and leaded lights, the perfect setting for rning coffee, lunch and afternoon tea. Owner Janet does the baking and her cakes have a devoted following. Try lemon meringue pie, the late Queen Mother's favourite te and walnut pudding, or Leek gingerbread from a ndred-year-old recipe. Greystones was winner of The Tea ild's Top Tea Room Award 2000, and The Tea Guild's Award of Excellence in 1999, 2001, 2002, 2003, 2004.

The Tea Guild's Award of Excellence 2005

RECOMMENDED IN THE AREA
Brindley Mill; Peak District National Park; Tittesworth Reservoir

Suffolk

Suffolk rusks are a bit like scones only drier, served with butter and sweet or savoury accompaniments. They are similar to Norfolk rusks, though aficionados have it that the Suffolk version is mixed a little richer and is consequently cut smaller. Suffolk, again like its neighbouring county Norfolk, has a creamy treacle tart without any breadcrumbs in it. Suffolk syllabub is another ancient sweet, a delightful concoction of lemon, sherry and cream. Greengages, a kind of green plum, were first grown in the 18th century by Sir William Gage in his orchards near Bury St Edmunds, and this unusual fruit is still popular in the area.

*H*intlesham Hall Hotel ★★★★ ⟐⟐⟐
Country house elegance in the heart of Suffolk

☎ 01473 652334
📠 01473 652463
✉ reservations@
   hintleshamhall.com
🌐 www.hintleshamhall.com

Map ref 4 - TM04

George Street, HINTLESHAM,
IP8 3NS
*4m W of Ipswich on A1071 to
Hadleigh & Sudbury.*
☕ Open daily; Tea served 3pm-6pm, but available at other times on request; Booking possible; Set tea price(s) Full Afternoon Tea £12.50; Chantilly Cream Tea £5.95; Seats 59; Guide dogs only; Parking 80
🛏 33 Rooms

Set in 175 acres of wonderful countryside, this Grade I listed Elizabethan manor house has Georgian additions, which include the wonderful façade. Afternoon tea is served in the cosy, intimate library, the elegant drawing room or the Garden Room. A selection of finger sandwiches (chicken and watercress, cured ham and grain mustard, cream cheese and chive, smoked salmon and capers) is followed by home-made scones with chantilly cream and preserves, and then chocolate chip and marmalade brownies. A good choice of teas is available, supplemented fruit and mint tisanes. Staff are friendly and professional, and you can work up an appetite with a stroll in the beautiful grounds or perhaps a round of golf.

RECOMMENDED IN THE AREA
Lavenham; Snape Maltings; Long Melford

Chocolate Chip and Marmalade Brownie

Recipe supplied by Hintlesham Hall Hotel
(page 128)

Makes 10 portions

Ingredients

2oz (50kg) broken plain chocolate
3oz (75g) unsalted butter
3oz (75g) dark chocolate
7oz (200g) caster sugar
3 medium eggs
4oz (112g) plain flour
½ teaspoon vanilla essence
1 tablespoon coarse cut marmalade, roughly chopped
icing sugar to dust

Method

You will need a 6in (15cm) square
cake tin and silicone paper.

Preheat oven to gas mark
2/300°F/160°C. (check)

Whisk the sugar and eggs together.
Melt the dark chocolate and butter,
and add to the sugar and eggs.
Add the vanilla essence.
Fold in the flour.
Add the broken chocolate and marmalade, and mix.
Line the cake tin with the silicone paper.
Pour the mixture into the tin and bake for 20–25 minutes until

lightly set.
Allow to cool, turn out and cut into
fingers.
Dust with icing sugar and serve.

*T*he Swan ★★★★ ◉◉

A picturesque setting for tea by the fire or the herb garden in a medieval market town

☎ 01787 247477
📠 01787 248286
✉ info@theswanatlavenham.co.uk
🌐 www.theswanatlavenham.co.uk

Map ref 4 - TL94

High Street, LAVENHAM, CO10 9QA
☕ Open daily; Tea served 3pm-5.30pm;
Closed 25-26 Dec; Set tea price(s) Suffolk
Cream Tea £7.50, Traditional Swan Tea
£13.95, Champagne Swan Tea £19.95;
Seats 50; No smoking; Parking 62
🛏 51 Rooms

A collection of listed buildings dating from the 14th century makes up this delightful hotel in the heart of historic Lavenham – the perfect stop-off after a stroll around the beautifully preserved streets and interesting shops. Tea is served in the lounge, the Garden Bar and the garden itself, and the all-day menu takes in morning coffee with toast and cakes; a range of sandwiches featuring honey roast Suffolk ham; and three set afternoon teas. There's the Suffolk Cream Tea with warm fruit scones, clotted cream and preserves; the Traditional Swan Tea, with finger sandwiches, chef's cake selection, and fruit scones with clotted cream and preserves, and the Champagne Swan Tea, with all the treats of the traditional tea served with a glass of champagne. The Swan has its own tea blend, offered alongside Earl Grey, Assam, Lapsang Souchong and Darjeeling, plus cappuccino, latte and espresso coffees. Herbal tea and tisanes are also available.

RECOMMENDED IN THE AREA

Long Melford; Bury St Edmunds; Flatford Mill

*F*lying Fifteens

seafront tea rooms by the award-winning South Beach

☎ 01502 581188
✆ 01502 586991

Map ref 4 - TM59

9a The Esplanade, LOWESTOFT,
NR33 0QG
*On South Beach seafront promenade,
between South Pier and Claremont
Pier, near Hotel Hatfield.*
Owner(s): Mrs Diana Knight
Open Spring Bank Hol to mid-Sep
daily except Mon; Easter-Spring Bank
Hol weekends only; Tea served
10.30am-5pm; Closed Mon winter;
Set tea price(s) Selection available;
Seats 33 + 50 outside;
No smoking; Dogs allowed in garden

These popular tea rooms benefit from full waitress service and a lovely garden overlooking the beach. All the food is home-cooked using the best ingredients, and chips are banned from the menu. Specialities include locally smoked salmon, honey roast Norfolk ham and, on Saturdays, fresh Cromer crab. There are no set meals, just a good choice of sandwiches, soup, omelettes, salads and cakes, with favourites such as strawberry scones, very large meringues and boozy fruitcake. The name 'Flying Fifteens' comes from a sailing boat designed by Uffa Fox in the 1940s, 'fifteen' relating to its 15-foot length. Teas, gifts and greeting cards are sold. Dogs permitted in the garden; parking close by.

The Tea Guild's Award
of Excellence 2005

RECOMMENDED IN THE AREA
*East Anglian Transport Museum; Pleasurewood Hills
Amusement Park; Suffolk Wildlife Park*

Surrey

Richmond Maids of Honour, sweet tartlets filled with an almond and lemon mixture, are thought to have originated at Hampton Court in the 16th century, where they were enjoyed by Henry VIII. There are many stories surrounding their origin, most of which involve the recipe being locked away in an iron box to maintain its exclusivity. Nevertheless, a recipe did appear in the second edition of *The Accomplisht Cook* by R May, published in 1665, and commercial production of Maids of Honour began in Richmond in 1750, by Thomas Burdekan at his shop in

Hill Street. Another old Surrey recipe is Crystal Palace pudding, from a Mrs Beeton collection published in 1909. This is a jellied custard turned out of a mould and decorated with glace cherries.

*H*askett's Tea & Coffee Shop

A well-cared for old building renowned for its teas

📞 01306 885833

Map ref 3 - TQ14

86B South Street, DORKING, RH4 2EW
Once in Dorking, proceed along High St to one way system, keep left, pass War Memorial, Haskett's on right opposite car park.
Owner(s): Mrs Margaret Garrett
☕ Open Mon-Sat 9am-5pm, Sun 11am-5pm; Closed Bank Holidays; Booking possible; Set tea price(s) Cream Tea £5.45, Haskett's Tea £6.75 No credit cards; Seats 32; No smoking; Air con

*P*oster art from the 1920s and 30s decorates the walls of this tea and coffee shop, but the building itself dates from the late 17th century, and a Grade II listing protects its architectural heritage. A cave with a 220ft well was discovered in the basement, now carefully sealed. A wide variety of tasty dishes is served, including liver and bacon, sausage and mash, and pasta bake, plus breakfasts, sandwiches, omelettes and salads. Afternoon tea is a high spot, with 25 varieties of tea to revisit or experiment with, as well as 10 different choices of coffees.

The Tea Guild's Award of Excellence 2005

RECOMMENDED IN THE AREA
Antiques in West Street; Box Hill for walking; Denbies wine estate

132

Ganache Chocolatier Tea Room

Belgian chocolatier and tea room on historic Ewell High Street

☎ 020 8 393 2128
✉ ganache@btconnet.com

Map ref 3 - TQ26

30 Ewell High Street, EWELL, KT17 1RW
A3 towards Guildford. Take exit for Tolworth Rise South into A240 (Kingston Road), right onto B2200 (London Road), straight on at lights.

☕ Open Mon-Sat 8.30am-6pm; Tea served all day; Closed Sun (except special occasions); Booking possible; Set tea price(s) £9.95; No smoking; Air con; No dogs

Ganache occupies a Grade II listed building in the village of Ewell and operates as both a tea room and chocolate shop, selling Belgian chocolates, French pastries, teas, home made jams, light lunches and sandwiches. The set afternoon tea comprises a selection of finger sandwiches, freshly baked scones with clotted cream and fruit preserve, and a variety of home-made cakes. The accompanying pot of tea is selected from a list of ten from around the world, including an exclusive house blend; ten herbal teas and infusions, and two specialities – a delicate Japanese Sench, and Formosa Pouchong, a green tea from China. Food is available all day, with pancakes, toast and pastries in the morning, and all day sandwiches and savouries such as a bagel with cream cheese and smoked salmon, or Welsh rarebit. There is always a good range of home made cakes and tea breads, made with organic free-range eggs. The tea room is available for private functions. An hour's free parking is permitted in two local car parks.

RECOMMENDED IN THE AREA

Epsom Races: Bourne Hall; Ewell village, the Mill walk

Almond and Mixed Peel Cake with Rum Syrup

Recipe supplied by Ganache (page 133)

Ingredients

7 eggs
7 tablespoons home-made breadcrumbs
7 tablespoons coarsely chopped almonds
2 teaspoons baking powder
¾ cup California raisins
1 cup mixed peel

For syrup:
1 cup water
4 tablespoons sugar
1 tablespoon rum

To decorate:
½ pint (275ml) whipping cream
2 tablespoons icing sugar

Method

Whisk eggs yolks until pale in colour, then add the breadcrumbs, almonds,
California raisins, peel and baking powder and stir with a spoon.
Whisk egg whites separately until soft peaks form.
Add egg whites to the yolk mixture and fold in gently until combined.

Line the base of a 9-inch (23cm) round cake tin with greaseproof paper and fold
in the cake.
Bake in preheated moderate oven at gas mark 3/325°F/170°C (fan 160 degrees)
for 40 minutes.

Prepare the syrup; combine water and sugar
in small saucepan, stir over heat until sugar
dissolves, and bring to a boil. Remove from
heat and add rum.

When cake is baked, pour the hot syrup
over it and leave to cool.

Prepare the whipped cream. Pour cream in
bowl, add icing sugar, few drops of vanilla
and whisk with an electric mixer until soft
peaks form. Once cake is cold, spread the
cream over it and decorate with toasted
almonds and mixed peel pieces.

*O*atlands Park Hotel ★ ★ ★ ★

Palatial premises in a country setting, but with easy access to the motorway network and airports

☎ 01932 847242
📠 01932 842252
✉ info@oatlandsparkhotel.com
🌐 www.oatlandsparkhotel.com

Map ref 3 - TQ06

146 Oatlands Drive, WEYBRIDGE, KT13 9HB
Through Weybridge High St to top of Monument Hill. Hotel on left.
☕ Open daily; Tea served 3pm-5pm;
Set tea price(s) £9.95; No dogs; Parking 140
🛏 144 Rooms

*T*his impressive property occupies the site of a former palace, Oatlands, built by King Henry VIII or Anne of Cleves and subsequently demolished round 1649. The galleried lounge provides an opulent setting; tea can also be taken on the terrace or out on the lawn overlooking the gardens. The comprehensive set tea provides assorted finger sandwiches and a choice of pastry or cake from the trolley. Alternatives include toasted teacakes and croissants.

RECOMMENDED IN THE AREA

Wisley RHS Gardens; Brooklands Museum; Hampton Court Palace

Thursley Common

Sussex

Sussex pond pudding is an old-fashioned steamed suet pudding, filling, delicious and very much the ultimate comfort food. To make the pudding the basin is lined with suet pastry and in this case a whole lemon, along with some butter and sugar, is carefully sealed inside the crust before steaming. When you cut into the cooked pudding, the 'pond' of buttery lemon sauce comes flooding out on to the plate until the pudding is swimming in the delightful goo.

Alternatively, for Sussex well pudding, dried fruit is included in the suet pastry crust, the pudding basin lined, and the cavity filled with butter and brown sugar before it is covered and steamed. This time, when the cooked pudding is cut into, out gushes a buttery 'well' of sauce to surround the pudding.

Seafood from the Sussex coast is a great teatime treat, with the likes of cod, herrings, mackerel, sprats, plaice, soles, turbot, shrimps, crabs, lobsters, oysters, mussels, cockles, whelks and periwinkles on offer, plus some first rate fish and chips. Locally smoked fish is also a speciality.

Shepherd's Tearooms

Ideal meeting place for tea lovers

☎ 01243 774761

Map ref 3 - SU80

35 Little London, CHICHESTER, PO19 1PL
Owner(s): Kenny & Suzanne Todd
☕ Open 9.15am-5pm Mon-Fri, 9am-5pm Sat, 10am-4pm Sun; Tea served all day; Closed 25, 26 Dec, 1 Jan, Bank Holidays; Booking possible; Seats 60; No smoking; Air con

The gentle buzz of contented conversation fills these cosy tea rooms throughout the day until closing time in the late afternoon. Polished wooden floorboards, pale walls and cosy tables create a welcoming atmosphere inside the Georgian building. A conservatory-style room at one end allows plenty of light to filter through to the main tea shop, where attentive waitresses serve the home-made food. Salads, sandwiches and at least seven rarebits are among the savoury choices, while early visitors can enjoy a cooked breakfast. The menu offers several loose-leaf teas and popular special blends, and traditional afternoon or cream teas along with scrumptious cakes and roulades.

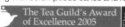
The Tea Guild's Award of Excellence 2005

RECOMMENDED IN THE AREA
Fishbourne Roman Palace; South Downs

The Grand Hotel ★★★★★ ◉◉

An impressive Victorian hotel overlooking the beach and sea

☎ 01323 412345
🖷 01323 412233
✉ reservations@ grandeastbourne.com
🖳 www.grandeastbourne.com

Map ref 4 - TV69

King Edward's Parade, EASTBOURNE, BN21 4EQ
On seafront, W of Eastbourne, 1m from railway station.
☕ Open daily; Tea served 3pm-6pm; Closed to non-residents 23-26 Dec; Booking required; Set tea price(s) £14-£19.50; Seats 120; No smoking areas; Parking 60
🛏 152 Rooms

Afternoon tea in the grand style can be taken in the hotel lounges, the Great Hall with its lofty ceiling and marble columns, or on the outdoor pool terrace in summer. For a special treat, tea can be enhanced with a glass of champagne, and on the last Sunday of the month (except June, July and December) the Palm Court strings play in the Great Hall at tea time. Full tea comprises a selection of teas, sandwiches, fresh scones with a choice of preserves and clotted cream, fresh strawberries or toasted teacake (according to season), and a selection of freshly made cakes and pastries. No dogs in public areas.

RECOMMENDED IN THE AREA
Walks on South Downs Way; Beachy Head Countryside Centre

Ashdown Park Hotel and Country Club

A magnificent house and grounds set in the heart of Ashdown Forest

☎ 01342 824988
🖷 01342 820206
📧 reservations@
**   ashdownpark.com**
🌐 www.ashdownpark.com

Map ref 3 - TQ43

Wych Cross, FOREST ROW,
RH18 5JR
A264 to East Grinstead, A22 to
Eastbourne. 2m S of Forest Row at
Wych Cross lights, turn left to
Hartfield. Hotel 0.75m on right.
☕ Open daily; Tea served 3pm-
5.30pm; Booking possible; Set tea
price(s) Afternoon Tea £17.50,
Champagne Tea £23.50; Seats 80;
Guide dogs only; Parking 200
🛏 106 Rooms

*T*he tradition of afternoon tea is proudly maintained at Ashdown Park Hotel, which offers an a la carte tea menu in the relaxed and elegant surroundings of the hotel's drawing rooms or outside on the terrace. Options range from simple tea and crumpets to a Champagne Tea – finger sandwiches, freshly baked scones served warm with clotted cream and a choice of preserves, and selection of cakes, tea breads and pastries – accompanie by a glass of chilled champagne and fresh strawberries wi cream. If you wish to treat someone else to afternoon tea a Ashdown Park, gift certificates are available at reception.

RECOMMENDED IN THE AREA
Wakehurst Place, Sheffield Park, Bluebell Railway

Gravetye Manor Hotel ★ ★ ★ ◍◍◍

Stone-built Elizabethan mansion with beautiful gardens

☎ 01342 810567
🖷 01342 810080
📧 info@gravetyemanor.co.uk
🌐 www.gravetyemanor.co.uk

Map ref 3 - TQ33

EAST GRINSTEAD, RH19 4LJ
M23 junct 10. A264 towards East
Grinstead. At 2nd rdbt take 3rd exit
(Turners Hill, B2028). 1 mile after
Turners Hill, L at fork in road. 100 yds
L again and then 1 mile on R.
☕ Open daily; Tea served 3pm-5pm
daily; Closed 25 -26 Dec, 1 Jan;
Booking required; Set tea price(s) £2(
Seats 8; No dogs; Parking 35
🛏 18 Rooms; S £100-£150,
D £150-£325

*O*ne of the first ever country house hotels, Gravetye Manor remains a shining example of its type. Delightful public rooms with oak panelling, fresh flowers and open fires provide the perfect setting for afternoon tea. Alternatively, in fine weather, guests can sit outside in the garden. An à la carte selection of sandwiches, cakes, biscuits and scones with cream and preserves is offered along with a choice of teas and coffees. The set afternoon tea includes all of the above plus Gravetye Spring Water. Please note that tea is served to non-residents by pri arrangement only. Gravetye preserves a available to purchase at reception.

RECOMMENDED IN THE AREA
Wakehurst Place; Chartwell; Hever Castl

The Pavilion

A period tea room on Eastbourne's seafront

☎ 01323 410374

Map ref 4 - TQ60

Royal Parade, EASTBOURNE,
BN22 7AQ
Owner(s): David Hiley
🍵 Open 10am-4pm in winter,
10am-5.30pm in summer; Tea served
all day; Closed 25 Dec, 1 Jan;
Booking possible (in winter); Set tea
price(s) £4.85, £7.50; Seats 90 + 40
outside; No smoking

A handsome tea room, reminiscent of the Victorian/Edwardian era, the Pavilion is located by the redoubt fortress looking out to sea. Traditionally uniformed waiting staff serve a choice of breakfast dishes, sandwiches, jacket potatoes, and hot dishes such as steak and ale pie, or fillet of salmon with prawn and lobster sauce. Two set teas are offered, a Sussex Cream Tea and a full Pavilion Afternoon Tea with sandwiches, scones and fancy cakes, both served with a pot of Pavilion Blend Tea. Facilities include a patio tea terrace, sun lounge and souvenir shop, and a pianist plays during summer afternoons and Wednesdays and weekends in the winter. Dogs are not allowed.

RECOMMENDED IN THE AREA

*'How we Lived Then' Museum of Shops &
Social History; Redoubt Fortress &
Museum; Wish Tower Puppet Museum*

The Tea Tree

15th century cottage tea room specialising in leaf tea and local produce

☎ 01797 226102
✉ theteatree@btconnect.com
🌐 www.the-tea-tree.co.uk

Map ref 4 - TQ91

12 High Street, WINCHELSEA,
TN36 4EA
On A259 between Hastings and Rye.
In centre of town beyond town gate.
Owner(s): Steve & Jo Turner
🍵 Open 10am-5pm; Tea served all
day; Closed Tue Feb-Dec; Set tea
price(s) from £5.25-£16.25; Seats 40 +
8 outside; No smoking; No dogs;
Street parking

This welcoming tea shop is located close to the medieval town gate in the centre of this historic Cinque Port. The tea shop once fronted the town forge and boasts a wealth of period features. Full of atmosphere, with a wide choice not only of teas but also lunches, using local organic and free range produce. Fresh salads, quiches, local crab, English wines, preserves, honey and chutneys feature in the shop. Don't miss Jo's giant cream-filled meringues and the freshly baked cakes and scones.

The Tea Guild's Award
of Excellence 2005

RECOMMENDED IN THE AREA

*Winchelsea Town Museum; Rye Harbour Nature Reserve;
Battle Abbey; Bodiam Castle; Great Dixter Gardens*

139

Brie and Bacon Quiche

Recipe supplied by The Tea Tree (page 139)

Ingredients

7oz (200g) self raising flour
1 teaspoon salt
3½oz (90g) butter (diced)
water to mix

brie slices
8 slices cooked bacon, chopped
½ pint (275ml) double cream
4 eggs plus 2 egg yolks
salt and pepper

Method

Sieve flour into a bowl, add salt and butter pieces. Rub in until the mix resembles fine breadcrumbs. Add water to make a dough.
Leave to rest in the refrigerator for 30 minutes.

Roll out the dough and line a quiche dish. Cover the pastry with baking parchment and fill with baking beans; bake blind at gas mark 4/350°F/180°C for 20 minutes. Take out beans and put to one side.

Lay the slices of brie around the dish and cover with the bacon. Mix together cream, eggs and yolks and season. Pour into the pastry case and cook for approximately 25–35 minutes, until browned and set.

Warwickshire

Warwickshire Truckle cheese has been made to the same recipe for 75 years by Fowlers of Earlswood in Warwickshire. The company also produces an oak-smoked version, a handmade blue cheese (Fowlers Forest Blue) and the Fowlers Warwickshire range of cheeses, flavoured with the likes of garlic and parsley, chilli, chive and onion, and cracked black pepper.

Warwick rarebit – a variation on Welsh rarebit – is a happy combination of toast topped with a sauce made from Warwickshire Truckle and one of Warwickshire's real ales.

Hand-made sausages are also a speciality in the county, and farmers' markets at Stratford-Upon-Avon, Kenilworth, Warwick, Royal Leamington Spa, Rugby, Southam and Coleshill are great places to pick up local fare.

A rdencote Manor Hotel, Country Club & Spa ★★★★ ◉◉

Privately owned hotel with extensive leisure and conference facilities

☎ 01926 843111
📠 01926 842646
✉ hotel@ardencote.com
🌐 www.ardencote.com

Map ref 3 - SP16

Lye Green Road, CLAVERDON, CV35 8LS
Off A4189 between Henley-in-Arden and Warwick. At Claverdon village green, follow sign to Shrewley. Hotel 1m on right.
🍴 Open daily; Light lunch & Afternoon Tea served 1pm-5.30pm; Set tea price(s) Afternoon Tea £8.50; Seats 12; No smoking; No dogs; Parking 150
🛏 75 Rooms; S £105, D £120-£235

*B*uilt as a gentleman's residence around 1860, the hotel is set in 45 acres of landscaped grounds. The Oak Room Lounge menu offers morning coffee, light lunches and afternoon tea. The set Ardencote Cream Tea comprises English sandwiches, dainty pastries, and scones with clotted cream and preserves. Sandwiches, club sandwiches, warm muffins and toasted teacakes are available à la carte, and tea choices include traditional English, Earl Grey, Darjeeling and herbal.

RECOMMENDED IN THE AREA
Warwick Castle; Hatton Country World; Stratford-upon-Avon

Wiltshire

Wiltshire has been at the centre of the bacon industry since the 18th century when many pigs were imported from Ireland to Bristol and were herded from the port along the drove roads to London. Calne was a regular resting point on the way, and so was assured a regular supply of pigs for curing. The traditional Wiltshire cure, dating back 300 years, produces a mildly flavoured, low-salt ham, ideal for sandwiches. The cooling of the meat using ice was introduced to Calne in 1856, enabling the Wiltshire cure to be applied on a large scale, providing bacon, ham and gammon for the whole country and for the export market.

The ever-popular lardy cake originally comes from Wiltshire; a bread dough stuffed with as much lard, fruit and sugar as the fancy takes the baker.

*T*he Rocking Horse Tea Rooms

An old coaching inn provides the delightful setting for the Rocking Horse Tea Rooms

☎ 01225 707272

Map ref 2 - ST96

The Kings Arms Hotel, Market Place, MELKSHAM, SN12 6EX
Owner(s): Mrs Patricia Bull
🍵 Open 9.30am-5pm daily; Tea served 2pm-5pm; Closed Bank Holiday Mondays; Booking possible; Set tea price(s) Cream tea £3.75, High Cream Tea £5.50; Seats 60-70; No smoking; Dogs allowed outside only; Parking 20

*A*t the Rocking Horse Tea Rooms, a large log fire burns in the winter and comfy easy chairs plus a large selection of teas are on hand to complement the delicious home-made pastries and cakes on offer. Meals include scrambled or poached eggs in the morning with toast and bacon; light lunches such as quiche, toasted sandwiches or jacket potatoes, and the likes of game casserole, mixed chargrill, and haddock in beer batter from the specials board. In the afternoon there is a set cream tea and high cream tea. Fresh milk and cream is supplie by a local dairy.

RECOMMENDED IN THE AREA
Chalfield Manor; Caen Hill Locks; Bowood House & Gardens; Lacock Abbey

The Bridge Tea Rooms

An award-winning tea shop where top quality teas are elegantly served in fine bone china cups

☎ 01225 865537

Map ref 2 - ST86

24a Bridge Street, BRADFORD-ON-AVON, BA15 1BY
Next to the old town bridge and lock-up.
Owner(s): Richard & Carole Whale
✆ Open Wed-Sat 10am-5pm, Sun 12pm-5.30pm; Tea served all day; Closed Mon & Tue, except BHs, when closed Tue & Wed; Booking possible (except at weekends and BHs); Set tea price(s) Famous Bridge Cream Tea £7.55, Bridge Full Afternoon Tea £18.95; Seats 48; No smoking; Guide dogs only; Car park opposite with 20 spaces

RECOMMENDED IN THE AREA

Saxon church; Tithe Barn (c.1341); Westwood Manor; City of Bath

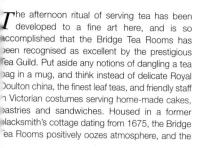

The afternoon ritual of serving tea has been developed to a fine art here, and is so accomplished that the Bridge Tea Rooms has been recognised as excellent by the prestigious Tea Guild. Put aside any notions of dangling a tea bag in a mug, and think instead of delicate Royal Doulton china, the finest leaf teas, and friendly staff in Victorian costumes serving home-made cakes, pastries and sandwiches. Housed in a former blacksmith's cottage dating from 1675, the Bridge Tea Rooms positively oozes atmosphere, and the classical music playing gently in the background sets a tranquil tone. Interesting light meals are also served throughout the day, but the famous Bridge Cream Tea is the main attraction here: expect large scones topped with Devonshire clotted cream and strawberry preserve, and a pot of one of 26 fine loose leaf teas presented to perfection in a beautiful teapot. Souvenir books and postcards are on sale.

The Tea Guild's Award of Excellence 2005

Soft Meringue Roulade

Recipe supplied by The Bridge Tea Rooms
(page 143)

Ingredients

10 egg whites
1 cup sugar
3 tablespoons cornstarch
1 cup shredded coconut

Method

Line a 10 x 15-inch Swiss roll tin with greaseproof paper. Preheat the oven to gas mark 2/300°F /150°C.

Whisk egg whites at full speed in an electric mixer. Add one-third of the sugar. Gradually add the remaining sugar and cornstarch until whites are firm.

Smooth the mixture into the tin and sprinkle with coconut. Bake for 10–15 minutes, or until top is completely golden brown and slightly risen. Leave to cool completely.

When cool, turn out onto a sheet of greaseproof paper, coconut side down.

Filling

2½ cups whipping cream
Vanilla essence
1 cup confectioner's sugar
1 pint fresh strawberries

Method

Mix cream at high speed with 3 drops of vanilla essence. Slowly sift in sugar. Mix until thick.

Spread filling over the baked meringue. Scatter on the sliced strawberries. Roll up into a roulade; chill. Slice to serve.

Manor House Hotel and Golf Club ★ ★ ★ ★ ◎◎

Stone-built manor house, dating back to the 14th century, surrounded by rolling Cotswold countryside

☎ 01249 782206
📠 01249 782159
📧 enquiries@manor-housecc.co.uk
🌐 www.exclusivehotels.co.uk

Map ref 2 - ST87

CASTLE COMBE, SN14 7HR
M4 junct 17. Take A350 to Bumpers Farm rdbt. R onto A420. Follow signs to Castle Combe, R onto B4039, through Yatton Keynell into Upper Castle Combe, L into Castle Combe. Through village, R immediately after the bridge.
🍴 Open daily; Tea served 2pm-5.30pm;
Set tea price(s) Cream Tea £5.50, Afternoon Tea £14.95; Seats 30;
Parking 100
🛏 48 Rooms

The hotel is set amid 365 acres of grounds, including an Italian garden, a Peter Alliss-designed 18-hole golf course, and well-kept lawns running down to the River Bybrook. Afternoon tea can be enjoyed in any one of the hotel's six lounges – cosy rooms with roaring fires in winter – or the leather furnished comfort of the Full Glass bar. In summer there is also the option of sitting outside in the beautiful garden. A selection of loose-leaf teas and herbal infusions is available and there is a choice between the cream tea or the full set afternoon tea, comprising sandwiches, freshly baked scones with

clotted cream and strawberry preserve, teacakes and Bath buns. Special events are a regular occurrence at Manor House Hotel, including afternoon teas for special occasions, such as Mother's Day and Easter, with a gift included. In summer there might be an afternoon tea party on the lawn with gifts for the children.

RECOMMENDED IN THE AREA

The Gallery on the Bridge (in Castle Combe); Castle Combe racetrack; Lacock Abbey

Worcestershire

The 'Blossom Trail' around the Vale of Evesham was devised so that motorists and cyclists could enjoy the glorious sights and scents of the orchards in bloom. Plum and damson blossoms are first out in March, followed by pears in April and finally apples in May. Worcester Black Pear trees, once a common sight, can still be seen in hedgerows and old gardens; they made excellent windbreaks for the orchards due to their large size. Worcester's city crest includes three Black Pears, and the city is also known for the 'Worcester Pearmain' – not a pear but an apple, a sweet and juicy fruit with red skin and white flesh, originating in 1873 and now a popular choice in sorbets. Local varieties of plum include the Evesham Wonder, the Pershore Yellow Egg and the Purple Pershore; Plum Day is celebrated annually on August Bank Holiday. The fruits are made into pies and preserves sold in the farmers' markets, and pressed to make still and sparkling ciders, perries and juices – another benefit of the apple and plum bonanza.

*T*he Lygon Arms ★★★★ ◉◉◉

Beautiful building full of historic character

T 01386 852255
F 01386 858611
E info@thelygonarms.co.uk
W www.thelygonarms.co.uk

Map ref 3 - SP13

High Street, BROADWAY, WR12 7DU
On High Street; Broadway is 6m from Evesham off A44.
🍽 Open daily; Tea served 2pm-6pm; Booking possible; Set tea price(s) English Afternoon Tea £13, Champagne Tea £20; Seats 70; Parking 152
🛏 69 Rooms

*B*uilt as an inn in 1532, the Lygon Arms is the archetypal country house hotel, with inglenook fireplaces, oak panelling and a wealth of antique furniture. It is located in the village of Broadway, surrounded by all the delights of the Cotswolds and by its own lovely garden. Tea is available in the lounges every day and at weekends in the baronial Great Hall restaurant. There is a set traditional afternoon tea and a champagne tea, both with home-made teacakes (a house speciality), scones and sandwiches, served on a three-tier cake stand. Other options are goats' cheese on toast and smoked salmon muffin.

RECOMMENDED IN THE AREA

Walks on the Cotswold Way; Broadway Tower & Animal Park

Lygon Arms Scones

Recipe supplied by The Lygon Arms
(page 146)

Ingredients

6oz (175g) organic plain flour
11oz (340g) unsalted butter
8oz (225g) unrefined caster sugar
4oz (110g) baking powder
½oz (10g) fine salt
2¼ pints (1 litre 130ml) cold full fat milk
5oz (150g) raisins

Method

Sieve the flour, salt and baking powder into a large bowl. Cut the butter
into small cubes and mix into the flour. When the mixture resembles fine
breadcrumbs, add the raisins and mix in the milk to make a smooth
dough. Roll out to ¾ inch and cut out circles with a plain or fluted scone
cutter.

Place on a lightly floured tray and bake in a moderately hot oven at gas
mark 4/ 350°F/180°C for 15–20 minutes until risen and golden. Remove
from oven and cool on a wire rack.

Serve at room temperature with plenty of clotted cream and strawberry
jam.

Some of the World's Best Teas

Speciality Teas:
- take their name from the plantation on which they are grown (usually referred to as single estate or single source teas)
- come from a particular area or country
- are blended for a particular time of day or occasion
- are blends to which flower, fruit, herb or spice flavourings have been added.

Taiwanese Teas

Formosa Oolong

When farmers from China's Fujian Province emigrated to the island of Formosa (now Taiwan) in the 1850s, they took with them their traditional methods of manufacturing tea. The best of Taiwan's oolongs are produced on the slopes of Mount Dung Ding. The infusion is orange-green and has a light, smooth taste. Drink without milk.

Japanese Teas

Sencha

This is the most common and popular of Japan's green teas. The freshly-picked leaves are first steamed and then fluffed by hot air and rolled, dried and polished to become flat, dark green, needle-like leaves. These brew quickly to give a pale yellow, very clear infusion that has a soft, herbal taste. No milk please.

Gyokuro

The very best of Japan's green teas requires special care and attention. The bushes are covered for about three weeks before being plucked, with canvas or reed mats to reduce the amount of light reaching the bushes as they grow. This means that the leaves produce more chlorophyll and have a much more concentrated sweet flavour than Sencha. Gyokuro is ground down to a fine powder to make 'matcha', which is then whisked into hot water and drunk during the famous Japanese Tea Ceremony. Drink without milk.

Teas from Sri Lanka (Ceylon)

Dimbula

Grown at 5,000 ft above sea level, Dimbula black teas a light, bright infusion and a crisp, strong flavour. Dimbula was one of the first areas of the island to be planted with tea after the demise of the coffee estates in the 1860s. Drink with or without milk.

Nuwara Eliya

Black teas from the hill country in the centre of the island are among Sri Lanka's finest. The even pieces of brown leaf give a rich golden liquor that has a lightly perfumed brisk flavour.

Uva

This fine flavoured black tea comes from the eastern slopes of the central mountains of Sri Lanka where the dry wind has a marked effect on the quality and character of the tea. Uva teas are bright in colour and have a dry, crisp taste. Enjoy with or without milk.

Yorkshire

Yorkshire has a rich heritage of traditional recipes, probably the best known of which is the Yorkshire pudding. A batter-based dish, rising to light, golden heights, Yorkshire pudding appears in many guises these days, from plate-sized filled Yorkshire pudding, through toad in the hole with sausages cooked in with the batter, to tiny and sophisticated canapés.

Yorkshire is another northern oat-growing area, where spicy, treacly, teatime treats include delicious sticky parkin, gingerbreads and brandy snaps. Parkin is also a customary Bonfire Night cake. Yorkshire teacakes are yeasted buns made with currants and candied peel and given a sweet sticky glaze. To serve, they should be split, toasted and laden with butter.

Wensleydale cheese is made in the area around Hawes in Wensleydale. White Wensleydale, using finely cut, lightly pressed curd, takes only three weeks to ripen and has a mild flavour and crumbly texture. Blue veined Wensleydale, far more pungent, takes six months to mature and is not unlike blue Stilton. White Wensleydale cheese is traditionally eaten with apple pie and fruitcake.

York ham is mild, lean and ideal for sandwiches. It is a more expensive product than other hams because of the special process of its preparation, which takes several months.

*T*he Georgian Tea Rooms

Quintessentially English tea rooms in one of the country's most complete Georgian streets

☎ 01262 608600
✉ GADandy@aol.com

Map ref 8 - TA16

56 High Street, Old Town, BRIDLINGTON, YO16 4QA
Owner(s): Diane Davison
☕ Open Mon-Sat 10am-5pm; Sun 10am-3pm; Tea served all day; Closed two weeks at Christmas; Booking possible; Prices: sandwiches from £2.50, cakes from £1; Seats 40; Smoking area; No dogs

A delightfully refreshing discovery in Bridlington's historic Old Town, the Georgian Tea Rooms occupies the ground floor of a Grade II listed building, and enhances its period charm with beautifully kept antique furniture. Diane Davison runs the business, with her cousin, Karen Peacock, taking care of the two upper floors of fine antique furniture, crafts, gifts, hand-made cards and antique jewellery – a browser's paradise. The large patio and garden to the rear are a surprise for first-time visitors; with its antique fountain, the garden is a great attraction in fine weather, with seating for a further couple of dozen people. The extensive menu offers excellent home-cooked food, freshly prepared from locally-supplied ingredients. Particular favourites include quiches, cakes and pastries, although the options range from breakfasts, through lunches with daily specials to even more cakes. A local artist painted this delightful view one Sunday afternoon *in situ*, wishing 'to capture that strong feeling of age and history together with that timeless image of teatime in England'. Family functions can be catered for. No dogs except guide dogs.

RECOMMENDED IN THE AREA

Bayle Gate Museum; Priory Church; High Street

Clark's Café
Family-run bakery and café halfway between York and Thirsk

☎ 01347 7821285

Map ref 8 - SE57

195 Long Street, EASINGWOLD, YO6 3JB
At south end of main street.
Owner(s): Hilary Ryder
☕ Open Mon-Fri 8am-4.30pm, Sat 8am-4pm; Tea served all day; Closed Sun & Bank Hols; Booking possible; Set tea price(s) £5; No cred cards; Seats 25; No smoking; Guide dogs only

Clarks was established by the proprietor's mother in 1925, who began by selling tea and home-baked scones to road repair men from Middlesborough. The café's display of colourful canal-ware reflects Gerald and Judy Clark's enthusiasm for narrow boats, and there's also a pretty garden with outside seating. Everything is made on the premises, and house specialities are the all-day breakfast, brunch, ploughman's/gamekeeper's lunch, and the set afternoon or cream tea. Other options range from chip butty, omelettes and sandwiches to tea time treats such as sausage rolls, teacakes vanilla slice and fruit cake served wit Wensleydale cheese. The Clarks have second tea room in the town centre. Guid dogs only. Parking provided.

RECOMMENDED IN THE AREA
City of York; Castle Howard; Beningbrough Hall

Clark's Tearooms
The Clarks' second tea room in town-centre Easingwold

☎ 01347 7823143

Map ref 8 - SE57

Market Place, EASINGWOLD, YO6 3AG
In town centre, opposite town hall.
Owner(s): Hilary Ryder
☕ Open Mon-Thu 10am-5pm, Fri-Sat 9.30am-5pm; Tea served all day; Closed Sun & Bank Hols; Booking possible; Set tea price(s) Afternoon Tea £5.20; No credit cards; Seats 48; No smoking; Guide dogs only

The original family bakery and café, situated on the edge of town, is complemented by this conveniently located tea room in Easingwold's Market Place. The menus are similar, with house specialities such as set afternoon tea, ploughman's/gamekeeper's lunch and cream tea, supplemented by daily specials from the blackboard. Enduringly popular are the range of sandwiches and toasties, light meals, pork pies, sausage rolls and home-made cakes. Local delicacies include traditional Yorkshire fruit cake with Wensleydale cheese, Yorkshire curd tart, and Clark's home-made toasted tea loaf. Home bakery products and pictures of the local area are also available to buy. Guide dogs only Free parking in town centre.

RECOMMENDED IN THE AREA
City of York; Castle Howard; North York Moors National Park

*B*ettys Café Tea Rooms

First of the six Bettys, opened in 1919

📞 01423 877300
📠 01423 877307
🌐 www.bettysandtaylors.co.uk
Map ref 7 - SE35
Parliament Square, HARROGATE,
HG1 2QU
Manager: June Wood
🍵 Open 9am-9pm daily; Tea served
all day; Closed 25-26 Dec, 1 Jan; Set
tea price(s) from £6.50; Seats 130;
No smoking; Air con

When young confectioner Frederick Belmont travelled from Switzerland to find his fortune he came to Harrogate accidentally – by catching the wrong train. He liked the place well enough to stay, married a local lass and opened the first Bettys. Today's unique Swiss/Yorkshire menu continues to reflect the heritage of the family business. Taylors of Harrogate is a sister company, importing and blending all the teas served, and each of the tea rooms has a shop selling teas, coffees, speciality breads, cakes, patisserie and chocolates, all hand made at Bettys Craft Bakery.

Cookery courses are also available at Bettys Cookery School, also in Harrogate. Children welcome; no dogs except guide dogs.

The Tea Guild's Award of Excellence 2005

RECOMMENDED IN THE AREA
Fountains Abbey; The Royal Pump Room Museum; RHS Garden at Harlow Carr

*B*ettys at RHS Garden Harlow Carr

Fabulous new setting for this famous family business

🕿 01423 505604
🌐 www.bettysandtaylors.co.uk

Map ref 7 - SE35

Crag Lane, HARROGATE, HG3 1QB
Off B6162 Otley Road.
Manager: Janet Parker
🍵 Open 9am-5.30pm daily; Tea
served all day; Closed 25-26 Dec, 1
Jan; Set tea price(s) from £6.50; Seats
224; No smoking; No dogs;
Large car park

Bettys is a Yorkshire institution, a third generation business which had just five outlets until the first new Bettys Café Tea Rooms for more than 30 years opened at the Royal Horticultural Society's 58-acre Harlow Carr Gardens. The existing building has been transformed with Lloyd Loom chairs, granite topped tables, palm trees, and a terrace overlooking the garden for fine weather. There is also a tea house in the middle of the gardens, plus a Bettys shop and delicatessen. The company buys and blends its own

(Taylors) teas from all over the world, and a set traditional or cream tea is available. A pianist plays on Sunday 10am-1pm.

RECOMMENDED IN THE AREA
RHS Garden Harlow Carr; Turkish Baths; Valley Gardens

*B*ettys Café Tea Rooms

A strikingly attractive tea room on the tree-lined Grove

☎ 01943 608029
🖷 01943 816723
🌐 www.bettysandtaylors.co.uk

Map ref 7 - SE14

32-34 The Grove, ILKLEY, LS29 9EE
Manager: Hazel Bone
🍽 Open 9am-5.30pm daily; Tea
served all day; Closed 25-26 Dec, 1
Jan; Set tea price(s) from £6.50; Seats
54; No smoking; Air con

*O*ne of the six famous Bettys, the Ilkley incarnation has a wrought-iron canopy and an extensive tea and coffee counter stacked with antique tea caddies. Other notable features are the specially commissioned stained-glass windows, depicting wild flowers from Ilkley Moor, and the large teapot collection. The tea room is a favourite with ramblers, tired, hungry and thirsty from a tramp across the moors. The guiding principle of Bettys' founder, Frederick Belmont, was that 'if we want things just right we have to make them ourselves', and Bettys Bakery still makes all the cakes, pastries, chocolates, breads and scones serve in the tea rooms. Children welcome; guide dogs only.

The Tea Guild's Award of Excellence 2005

RECOMMENDED IN THE AREA
Ilkley Moor; Haworth Parsonage; National Museum of Photography, Film and Television

---

*T*he Star at Scampston

Innovative operation within the walled garden at Scampston Hall

☎ 01944 759000
✉ starinn@btopenworld.com
🌐 www.thestaratharome.co.uk

Map ref 8 - SE77

Walled Garden, Scampston Hall,
MALTON, YO17 8NG
*On A64 between Scarborough and
Malton, near Rillington.*
Owner(s): A & J Pern
🍽 Open Tue-Sun & Bank Hols; Tea
served 10am-5pm; Closed Mon; Boo
in advance for groups of 6 or more;
Prices: sandwiches from £4, cakes &
puddings from £1; Seats 70;
No smoking; No dogs; Parking 100

*T*his airy modern establishment is run by Andrew and Jacquie Pern of the Star Inn at Harome. Coffee, teas and light lunches are served, using produce from the gardens. Local ingredients star in an interesting range of sandwiches: roasted rare Middle Baxton beef, blue Wensleydale rarebit, Helmsley ham, and Harome village eggs. Eccles cakes and parkin with rhubarb echo the regional theme. A choice of teas and coffees is offered alongside some appetising smoothies, juices and old fashioned fizzy pop. Items such as home-made pickles, jams, cookery books, crockery and paintings are available for sale, and cooker courses and demonstrations are a feature in a specially designed kitchen.

RECOMMENDED IN THE AREA
Scampston Hall & Walled Garden; Castle Howard; Wolds Way Lavender

Baked Ginger Parkin with Rhubarb Ripple Ice-cream and Hot Spiced Treacle

Recipe supplied by The Star at Scampston (page 154)

Parkin

Makes an 8in (20cm)
square cake

Ingredients

4oz (110g) self raising flour
pinch of salt
2 teaspoons ground ginger
½ teaspoon ground nutmeg
½ teaspoon mixed spice
3oz (75g) oatmeal
6oz (175g) golden syrup
2oz (50g) black treacle
4oz (110g) butter
4oz (110g) soft brown sugar
1 egg (beaten)
2 dessertspoons milk

Method

Preheat oven to gas mark 1/275°F/ 140°C.
Sieve together the flour, salt, ginger, nutmeg
and mixed spice.
Mix in the oatmeal.
Melt the syrup, treacle, butter and sugar and
simmer, but do not boil. Then stir in the dry
mix and blend together.
Add the beaten egg and milk to the mixture to
create a soft, almost pouring consistency. Pour
into a greased tin and bake for 1¼ hours until
firm in centre. When cooked, allow to stand for
¼ hour before turning out.
The parkin can be served immediately, but will
improve with age if kept in an airtight container;
the best flavour will be achieved by storing it for
three weeks.

Rhubarb Ripple Ice-cream

Makes 8 servings to accompany the pudding

Ingredients

7fl oz (200ml) full fat milk
9fl oz (250ml) double cream
½ vanilla pod, split and scraped out
6 egg yolks
4oz (110g) caster sugar
9oz (250g) rhubarb, chopped and lightly stewed
2oz (50g) sugar approx, to sweeten

Method

Use the first five ingredients to make a crème anglaise mix and cool
down and churn in an ice-cream machine.
Meanwhile, sieve the stewed rhubarb and reduce down the juices.
Make sure this is cool, then add to the ice-cream. When nearly, frozen,
add the pulp to the ice-cream to give e ripple effect, then turn machine off.

Hot Spiced Treacle

Mix together 7oz (200ml) golden syrup, ½fl oz (10ml) cider and ½ teaspoon
ground mixed spice, and warm through.

*B*ettys Café Tea Rooms

The most northerly of the six Bettys tea rooms

☎ 01609 775154
🖷 01609 777552

Map ref 8 - SE39

188 High Street, NORTHALLERTON, DL7 8LF
Manager: Lindsay Judd
☕ Open Mon-Sat 9am-5.30pm
Sun 10am-5.30pm; Tea served all day;
Closed 25 & 26 Dec, 1 Jan; Set tea
price(s) from £6.50; Seats 58;
No smoking; Air con

*T*he Northallerton branch of Bettys is a sunny golden room, intimate in scale, decorated with art deco mirrors and antique teapots. Two set teas are offered: a Yorkshire Cream Tea with two sultana scones, butter, strawberry preserve and Yorkshire clotted cream, or the Bettys Traditional Afternoon Tea with a choice of sandwich, a sultana scone with butter, preserve and cream, followed by a choice of Yorkshire curd tart or chocolate éclair. In both cases the tea in the pot is Bettys Tea Room Blend of top class African and Assam teas. Children are welcome and good facilities are provided to keep them fed, cleaned, changed and entertained. Guide dogs only.

The Tea Guild's Award of Excellence 2005

RECOMMENDED IN THE AREA
North York Moors; Flamingo Land; Rievaulx Abbey

*S*winton Park ★ ★ ★ ★ ❀❀❀

Castle hotel with 200 acres of parkland, gardens and lakes

☎ 01765 680900
🖷 01765 680901
✉ enquiries@swintonpark.com
🌐 www.swintonpark.com

Map ref 7 - SE28

MASHAM, HG4 4JH
From A1 north of Ripon, B6267 to Masham. Follow signs through town centre.
☕ Open daily; Tea served 3pm-6pm;
Booking possible; Set tea price(s)
Cream Tea £6.50, Traditional
Wensleydale Tea £6.50, Full Afternoon
Tea £12; Seats 25; No smoking;
No dogs; Parking 50
🛏 30 Rooms

*T*he ancestral home of the Cunliffe-Lister family, Swinton Park dates from the 17th century but was extended in the Victorian and Edwardian periods. The castle is surrounded by the family estate in beautiful countryside – moorland, dales and rivers – bordering the Yorkshire Dales National Park. The bar and lounge menu includes sandwiches, light meals and desserts, plus a range of iced teas, leaf teas and freshly ground coffees. Three set teas are served in the lounge: a cream tea, Wensleydale tea (Yorkshire tea with locally made fruit cake and Wensleydale cheese), and full afternoon tea with sandwiches, cakes and scone with clotted cream and preserves.

RECOMMENDED IN THE AREA
Fountains Abbey; Newby Hall; Castle Howard

Swinton Ginger Parkin

Recipe supplied by Swinton Park
(page 156)

Serves 8

Ingredients

4oz (110g) self raising flour
½oz (10g) ground ginger
1oz (2.5g) ground nutmeg
3½oz (80g) oatflakes
6½oz (185g) golden syrup
1½oz (40g) black treacle
3½oz (100g) unsalted butter
4oz (110g) brown soft sugar
2 teaspoons milk

Method

Preheat oven to gas mark 2/300°F/150°C.
Butter a 10 inch (25cm) cake tin.
Mix flour, ginger and nutmeg together in bowl and add oatflakes.
Heat treacle and syrup until runny, mix in brown sugar and butter and simmer over a low heat.
Stir flour mix into the treacle mix.
Mix in beaten egg and milk.
Pour into the buttered tin and bake for 1 hour, until firm.
Leave to cool and cut up into squares.

*E*lizabeth Botham & Sons

Famous tea rooms specialising in Victorian recipes and fine teas

☎ 01947 602823
✉ mj@botham.co.uk
Ⓦ www.botham.co.uk

Map ref 8 - NZ91

35/39 Skinner Street, WHITBY, YO21 3AH
Owner(s): Michael & Sarah Jarman
🏆 Open 9.30am-4.40pm (5pm May-Oct);
Closed Sun (Jun-Sep); Tea served all day;
Closed Sun & Mon (Sep-May), 25-26 Dec, 1
Jan, Bank Hols; Booking possible; Set tea
price(s) £3.60-£6.50; Seats 100;
No smoking; Guide dogs only

RECOMMENDED IN THE AREA

Whitby Abbey; Captain Cook Museum; Pannett Museum

*T*he invitation to take tea at Botham's is an irresistible one involving wonderful cakes and pastries made from Victorian recipes, and a huge range of rare and fine teas. Botham's was established in 1865 by Elizabeth Botham and is still run by her great-grandchildren. The first-floor tearooms offer scones and teabreads, cream teas and toasts, special lunch of the day, jacket potatoes, salads and sandwiches. Afternoon te comes with the house Resolution Tea, or you can fi China Yunnan, Java Gunpowder and Darjeeling Fir Flush Bannockburn and many others on the menu, if your taste is for coffee, a variety of classic blends.

The Tea Guild's Award
of Excellence 2005

Whitby Spice Loaf

Recipe supplied by Elizabeth Botham & Sons Ltd
(page 158)

Ingredients

2lb (900g) plain flour
pinch of salt
1oz (25g) baking powder
½ teaspoon grated nutmeg
4oz (110g) butter, diced
4oz (110g) lard, diced
1lb (450g) soft brown sugar
1lb (450g) currants
8oz (225g) sultanas
4oz (110g) candied peel
2 eggs, beaten
1 pint (575ml) milk

Method

Preheat oven to gas mark 3/325°F/170°C.

Sift flour, salt, baking powder and nutmeg together in a bowl.
Add the butter and lard and rub in with the fingertips, until the mixture
resembles fine breadcrumbs. Stir in sugar, currants, sultanas
and candied peel.

Add the eggs, a little at a time, followed by the milk. Mix to a fairly
soft consistency. Divide the mixture between two well greased 3lb (1.3kg)
loaf tins and bake for 1½–2 hours.

Serve the loaf sliced and buttered.

*B*ettys Café Tea Rooms

Bettys in York – a flagship café in the heart of the city

☎ 01904 659142
🖷 01904 627050
🌐 www.bettysandtaylors.co.uk

Map ref 8 - SE65

6-8 St Helen's Square, YORK,
YO1 8QP
Manager: Paula Kaye
🍴 Open 9am-9pm daily;
Tea served all day; Closed 25-26 Dec
1 Jan; Set tea price(s) from £6.50;
Seats 213; No smoking; Air con

*I*n 1936 Frederick Belmont, Bettys founder, travelled on the maiden voyage of the *Queen Mary*, during which time he was planning a new café in York. The luxury liner provided the required inspiration, and the ship's interior designers were commissioned to recreate the magnificent panelling, pillars and mirrors in the elegant new premises. Favourite dishes include Swiss rösti, Alpine macaroni, Masham sausages and Yorkshire Rarebit, plus a fine selection of cakes, patisserie and desserts. Children have always been welcome, and there's 'Little Rascals' menu, books, toys, organ baby food and both gents' and ladie baby-changing facilities. A café pian enhances the atmosphere during th evenings. Guide dogs only.

The Tea Guild's Award
of Excellence 2005

RECOMMENDED IN THE AREA
York Minster; Castle Howard; York Dungeon

*L*ittle Bettys

A listed building in medieval Stonegate close to the Minster

☎ 01904 622865
🖷 01904 640348
🌐 www.bettysandtaylors.co.uk

Map ref 8 - SE65

46 Stonegate, YORK, YO1 8AS
Manager: Paula Kaye
🍴 Open Sun-Fri 10am-5.30pm,
Sat 9am-5.30pm; Tea served all day; Closed
25-26 Dec, 1 Jan; Set tea price(s) from £6.50;
Seats 65; No smoking; Air con

*T*here are six versions of Bettys, two of them in York, and this is the smallest of all. The café is reached via a flight of winding stairs and has a delightful interior characterised by wooden beams and roaring fires. Hot dishes, speciality sandwiches and an extensive range of cakes and patisserie are served, with the Yorkshire Fat Rascal as a house speciality – a large fruity scone with citrus peel, almonds and cherries. Teas are supplied by Bettys' sister company, family tea merchants Taylors of Harrogate, including some UK exclusives. Bettys is famously family-friendly, and children are made particularly welcome. Guide dogs only.

The Tea Guild's Award
of Excellence 2005

RECOMMENDED IN THE AREA
York Minster; Jorvik Viking Centre; National Railway Museum

*B*ullivant of York

All-day home-cooked fare in a city centre location

☎ 01904 671311
Map ref 8 - SE65
5 Blake Street, YORK, YO1 2QJ
Manager: Carolyn Haynes
⏰ Open Mon-Fri 9.30am-5pm, Sat
9am-5pm, Sun 11am-5pm
(summer/autumn); Closed 25-26 Dec;
Booking possible; Set tea price(s) £4.50;
Seats 43 plus 14 outside; Guide dogs only

A good choice of teas, coffees and herbal infusions is available at this friendly tea room, which has fine weather seating in the courtyard outside. The menu lists an extensive selection of meals, sandwiches and snacks prepared to order, plus an enticing range of home-made desserts. Set teas include a traditional high tea, cream tea and the speciality Chocolate Heaven – chocolate chip scone with Yorkshire clotted cream and luxury praline chocolate spread served with hot chocolate. The high tea offers baked beans on toast or boiled egg with toasted soldiers as an alternative to sandwiches. Home-made jams and chutneys are available to buy.

RECOMMENDED IN THE AREA

York Minster; National Railway Museum; The Shambles

Middlethorpe Hall Hotel, Restaurant & Spa ★ ★ ★ ◉◉

William III house set in beautifully restored gardens and parkland

☎ 01904 641241
📠 01904 620176
✉ info@middlethorpe.com
🌐 www.middlethorpe.com

Map ref 8 - SE65

Bishopthorpe Road, Middlethorpe, YORK, YO23 2GB
☕ Open daily; Tea served 3pm-5.30pm; Closed 24-25 Dec & 31 Dec; Booking preferred; Set tea price(s) Full Afternoon Tea £14.50, Champagne Afternoon Tea £22.45; Seats 25; No smoking in the Library; Guide dogs only; Parking 70
🛏 29 Rooms

RECOMMENDED IN THE AREA

York Minster; Rievaulx Abbey; Castle Howard

Once the home of the famous diarist Lady Mary Wortley Montagu, Middlethorpe Hall was built in 1699, and while it is set in 20 acres of grounds it is still conveniently located for the city of York. Afternoon tea can be taken in the drawing room or library – both very distinguished rooms – or out on the terrace in summer. Nineteen different teas are offered from the Taylors Harrogate fine selection, and tea time treats take finger sandwiches, toasted teacakes and fruit cake, but best of all are the home-made pastries and scones. Special events include a classical afternoon tea recital as part of the Middlethorpe Music Encounters.

Robin Hood's Bay

Scotland

Oats were long a staple of the Scottish diet and this is reflected in foods still widely served today, like Scottish oatcakes, which are crisp biscuits, good with cheese or sweet preserves, and cranachan, a delicious mixture of toasted oatmeal, cream and soft fruit like raspberries and strawberries, which are grown in abundance in Scotland. Whisky, Scottish liqueurs and heather honey are frequently added to dishes, including fruitcakes, desserts and tablet to impart a Scottish flavour. Tablet is a sweetie made from sugar, butter and condensed milk, a bit like fudge but slightly harder. Scotland has a fabulous range of tea breads, cakes and biscuits. Among these are Scots pancakes, a batter mix fried on a griddle and served with butter, and the satisfying potato scone. Bannocks are a kind of oat-based scone cooked on a griddle, but there are some wide variations. Selkirk bannock is a sweet fruit bread, cooked as a loaf and served sliced with butter, while Pitcaithy

bannock is more like a shortbread with almonds and candied peel. Scotland is renowned for its delicious shortbread, and in some remote parts of the country it served as bride's cake. As the bride entered her new home, the decorated shortbread would be broken over her head and the pieces distributed among her friends. The classic Scottish fruitcake, Dundee cake, is rich and buttery, decorated with circles of blanched almonds, while black bun is traditional Hogmanay fare, a mixture of fruit and spices cooked as a loaf in a pastry casing. Aberdeen butteries are bread rolls with a very high butter content, a little like croissants in some respects, and are generally available all over Aberdeenshire. Favourite savouries include smoked salmon, Arbroath smokies (lightly smoked haddock generally flaked and served with a creamy sauce), and Forfar bridies, which are meat pies a bit like Cornish pasties in appearance.

*T*he Coach House Coffee Shop

A village coffee shop on the western shore of Loch Lomond

☎ **01436 860341**
📠 **01436 860336**
✉ **enquiries@**
   lochlomondtrading.com
🌐 **www.lochlomondtrading.com**

Map ref 9 - NS39

Loch Lomond Trading Co Ltd, LUSS,
G83 8NN
Owner(s): Rowena Groves
☕ Open daily; Tea served
10am-5pm; Booking possible;
Seats 150; No smoking

*L*uss provides the delightful setting for Gary and Rowena Groves' café/gift shop, where you are likely to be welcomed by a log fire, Gaelic music and a traditionally kilted proprietor. It is called a coffee shop, but has plenty to offer the tea connoisseur. Light meals and snacks with a Scottish flavour are served in generous portions, and home-made soup, home-baked rolls and home-produced free range eggs are featured. Speciality fruit cakes are laced with malt whisky or baked with ale and studded with crystallised ginger. Goods available for sa: include teas, coffees, teapots, confectionary and cake: Parking is available in the main village car park.

RECOMMENDED IN THE AREA

Loch Lomond Cruises; Luss Glen; Ben Lomond & Ben Arthur (local munros)

---

*T*he Tea Room

A welcome oasis of calm in the middle of the busy Royal Mile

☎ **07771 501679**
✉ **trish@the-tea-room.info**
🌐 **www.the-tea-room.info**

Map ref 10 - NT27

158 Canongate, Royal Mile, EDINBURGH,
EH8 8DD
Situated on the Royal Mile, near the Palace c Holyroodhouse and the new Scottish Parliament.
Owner(s): Trish Noon
☕ Open daily 10am-4pm; Tea served all day; Closed 25 Dec; Booking possible for groups only; No credit cards; Seats 22; No smoking; Guide/Assist dogs only

*Y*ou can have your tea leaves read eve Thursday between 2 and 5pm at this calm te room with linen tablecloths and watercolours k local artists decorating the walls. All sorts lunchtime dishes are listed on the menu, from soup to toasted sandwiches and filled baked potatoe and delectable desserts. When it comes to tea time you can choose a traditional afternoon version or cream tea, with the scrumptious home-bake scones and interesting range of cakes to remind yc of what afternoons are for.

The Tea Guild's Award
of Excellence 2005

RECOMMENDED IN THE AREA

Scottish Parliament; Palace of Holyroodhouse; The People's Story

*G*eorge Inter-Continental ★★★★

Sumptuous Adam hotel with a choice of luxurious teas and champagne for added sparkle

☎ 0131 225 1251
📠 0131 226 5644
✉ edinburgh@interconti.com
🌐 www.edinburgh.intercontinental.
com

Map ref 10 - NT27

19-21 George Street, EDINBURGH,
EH2 2PB
Open daily; Tea served 3pm-5pm;
Booking recommended; Set tea price(s)
Traditional tea £11.50, Champagne tea
£17.50; Seats Lounge 20, Restaurant 40;
Air con; Guide dogs only; Parking 20
195 Rooms; S £75-£180, D £85-£240

'*T*he George' is located in the heart of the shopping and business centre of Edinburgh, on George Street, 'the Bond Street of the north', running parallel to Princes Street, the city's main thoroughfare. It is a long established hotel, designed by Robert Adam 200 years ago, with splendid public areas and a handsome façade with listed building status. The marble floored foyer makes a great first impression, and original features such as intricate plasterwork and chandeliers are retained throughout. Afternoon tea is served in both the lounge and Le Chambertin restaurant, and three options are available: the traditional Scottish tea, the Georgian and the à la carte. The traditional tea includes finger sandwiches, French pastries, Dundee cake, and a scone with strawberry preserve and clotted cream, while the Georgian adds a glass of Mercier Champagne and millionaires shortbread. Specialities include Drambuie-marinated gravadlax, and Belgian waffles with wild berry compôte and cream. Parking is provided for residents only.

RECOMMENDED IN THE AREA
Jenners department store; Edinburgh Castle; Scottish National Portrait Gallery

Drambuie Marinated Gravadlax

Recipe supplied by
The George Inter-Continental, Edinburgh
(page 165)

Ingredients

4.4lb (2kg) salmon fillet, skin on
1 cup sugar
⅓ cup salt
4fl oz (2.25ml) Drambuie
1oz (25g) juniper berries
2 tablespoons chopped dill
1 teaspoon cracked black pepper corns
1 cup coarse Arran mustard
2 cups crème fraiche

Method

Wash the salmon fillet under cold water and dry with a paper towel. Roast the juniper berries slightly in a dry pan or under the grill for a minute, to release the aromas and crush them a little. Mix the salt. Sugar, dill, pepper and juniper berries all together in a bowl.

Lay the salmon on sheet of greaseproof paper, skin side down. Brush ⅔ of the Drambuie over the salmon and sprinkle generously with the seasoning mixture. Fold the paper from all sides over the salmon and wrap tightly in cling film. Turn onto a tray (skin side up), place a weight on it and leave for 36 hours.

Remove paper and cling film and brush on the remaining Drambuie. Refrigerate for 2 hours.

Slice thinly and arrange on a plate. Mix the crème fraiche with the mustard, and serve with the salmon.

Buying, Storing and Brewing Tea

When you buy packaged tea, make sure that packets and tins are undamaged and that any wrapping is intact. It is important that the tea has been kept in air-tight conditions in order to preserve flavour and quality.

When buying loose-leaf tea, it is worth remembering that tea keeps best at the retailer's shop when stored in large canisters that have air-tight lids with a strong seal. Tea should not be stored in glass, and is best in cool, dry conditions.

The leaf should look dry and even and all the pieces of leaf should be approximately the same size. An uneven blend that has leaves of varying particle size can cause problems when brewing as the different sized pieces of leaf will release their flavour and colour at different rates, thereby giving an unbalanced overall flavour and quality.

At home, always store leaf and bagged tea in an air-tight container with a tightly-fitting lid and keep in a cool dry place away from other strong flavours and smells, as tea easily absorbs other flavours.

Brewing a good cup of tea

• Always use good quality loose leaf or bagged tea

• Always fill the kettle with freshly drawn cold water

• When brewing black and oolong teas, allow the water to reach boiling point before pouring on to the leaves

• When brewing green tea, boil the water and then allow it to cool slightly before pouring on to the leaves

• Measure the tea carefully into the pot: use one tea bag or one rounded teaspoon of loose tea for each cup to be served

• Allow the tea to brew for the correct number of minutes. Small leafed black tea normally needs 2-3 minutes; larger leafed black tea needs 3-5 minutes; oolong teas need 5-7 minutes; green teas need 1-3 minutes. Where possible, follow instructions on packets or test each tea to find the number of minutes that suits you.

Loch Lomond

*T*he Willow Tearoom

Stylish modern tea rooms in the heart of the city

☎ 0141 332 0521
✉ sauchiehallstreet@
  willowtearooms.co.uk
🌐 www.willowtearooms.co.uk

Map ref 9 - NS66

217 Sauchiehall Street, GLASGOW, G2 3EX
In city centre.
Owner(s): Anne Mulhern
☕ Open daily; Tea served 9am-4.30pm
Mon-Sat, 11am-4.15pm Sun; Closed 25-26
Dec, 1-2 Jan; Booking possible; Set tea
price(s) Afternoon tea £8.95, cream tea
before 12pm £2.95; Seats 89; No smoking
areas; Air con; Guide dogs only

Kate Cranston. The food served here is more than
match for the striking settings, and afternoon tea is
popular ritual with the city's many tourists. Enjoy
selection of sandwiches, scones with preserves an
cream, a choice of cakes and a delicious pot of loos
leaf tea or a decent coffee.

*S*tunning modern designs including tall silver chairs
in futuristic styles and mirrored friezes are a talking
point when guests first enter these smart tearooms.
Located above a jewellery shop in this famous street,
The Willow goes back to 1903 when Charles Rennie
Mackintosh created a series of tea shops for owner

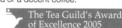
The Tea Guild's Award
of Excellence 2005

RECOMMENDED IN THE AREA
*Pollock House; Glasgow Science Centre; Glasgow
School of Art*

Willow Tea Rooms

Stunning and beautiful tea room with food to match

☎ 0141 204 5242
✉ buchananstreet@
willowtearooms.co.uk
🌐 www.willowtearooms.co.uk

Map ref 9 - NS66

97 Buchanan Street, GLASGOW,
G1 3HF
In city centre.
Owner(s): Anne Mulhern
🍽 Open daily; Tea served
9am-4.30pm Mon-Sat, 11am-4.15pm
Sun; Closed 25-26 Dec,
1-2 Jan; Booking possible; Set tea
price(s) Afternoon tea £8.95, cream
tea before 12pm £2.95; Seats 88;
Air con; Guide dogs only

The Willow theme of placing strikingly beautiful furniture against a calm and tasteful background works as well here as at the sister tea shop in Sauchiehall Street. The same architect, Charles Rennie Mackintosh, was responsible for the designs at the turn of the last century, when he created a series of tea shops for Kate Cranston. Upstairs is the blue Chinese Room with small furniture, while downstairs the amazing high-backed chairs are impossible to ignore. Tea is something of a distraction, though, with its classic afternoon selection served with a good range of fine teas. There are plenty of savoury and sweet choices throughout the day too.

RECOMMENDED IN THE AREA
*House for an Art Lover; The Lighthouse;
Clydebuilt*

Abbey Cottage Tea Rooms

Attractive cottage tea rooms next to Sweetheart Abbey

☎ 01387 850377
F 01848 200536
✉ morag@
abbeycottagetearoom.com
🌐 www.abbeycottagetearoom.
com

Map ref 5 - NX97

26 Main Street, New Abbey,
DUMFRIES, DG2 8BY
*From Dumfries take A710 Solway
Coast Road. Abbey Cottage is beside
the car park of Sweetheart Abbey.*
Owner(s): Morag McKie &
Jacqui Wilson
🍽 Open daily Apr-Oct; Sat & Sun
Nov, Dec & Mar; Tea served all day;
Closed Jan & Feb; Booking possible;
Prices: Sandwiches from £2.50; cakes
from £1.20; Seats 56 plus outside; No
smoking; Guide dogs only; Parking 60

Quality is the watchword at this highly acclaimed tea rooms, where morning coffee, light lunches and afternoon teas are all freshly prepared on the premises, using the best of ingredients from mainly local suppliers. Home-made pâtés, home-made organic bread and organic farmhouse cheeses are a speciality. Abbey Cottage also has its own well-stocked gift shop.

RECOMMENDED IN THE AREA
*Sweetheart Abbey; New Abbey Corn Mill;
Shambellie House Museum of Costume*

The Tea Guild's Award
of Excellence 2005

Date Slices

Recipe supplied by Abbey Cottage Tea Rooms
(page 169)

Ingredients

For the base:
8oz (225g) plain flour
8oz (225g) margarine
6oz (175g) semolina
4oz (110g) caster sugar

For the filling:
1 block of dates
4 dessertspoons water
1 dessertspoon runny honey
1 dessertspoon lemon juice

Method

Mix together the ingredients for the base and press into a greased swiss roll tin, retaining some for topping.

To make the filling, soften the ingredients in a pan or in a microwave. Mix with a potato masher and spread over the base.

Sprinkle the remaining mixture on top and bake for 30 minutes at gas mark 3/325°F/170°C

Kind Kyttock's Kitchen

Traditional Scottish tea rooms in a historic setting

☎ 01337 857 477
✉ q-dalrymple@yahoo.co.uk

Map ref 10 - NO20

Cross Wynd, FALKLAND, KY15 7BE
Owner(s): Bert & Quentin Dalrymple
☕ Open Tue-Sun 10.30am-5.30pm; Tea
served all day; Closed Mon, 25 Dec-5 Jan;
Booking possible; Seats 74; No smoking;
Guide dogs only; Car park opposite,
15 spaces

The picturesque village of Falkland is dominated by Falkland Palace, the hunting palace of the Stuart monarchs, and close by is Kind Kyttock's tea rooms, where all the produce is made on the premises. A wide variety of snacks, soups, sandwiches, salads and sweets is served, and the set afternoon tea includes a pot of tea together with a scone and pancake, plus a choice of home-made preserves and two home-made cakes. Children are welcome and high chairs are provided. Free parking is available opposite the tea room, and you can book ahead for tea. A small selection of items is offered for sale.

RECOMMENDED IN THE AREA
Falkland Palace; Falkland Estate for country walks; Golf at St Andrews

The Tea Guild's Award
of Excellence 2005

The Old Course Hotel, Golf Resort & Spa ★★★★★ ◉◉◉

Traditional afternoon tea, with a surprising variation

☎ 01334 474371
📠 01334 477668
✉ reservations@
   oldcoursehotel.co.uk
🌐 www.oldcoursehotel.co.uk

Map ref 10 - NO51

ST ANDREWS, KY16 9SP
Close to A91 on outskirts of the city.
☕ Open daily; Tea served
2.30pm-4.30pm daily; Booking
recommended; Set tea price(s)
Traditional Afternoon Tea £13.50,
Champagne Afternoon Tea £21,
Chocolate Afternoon Tea £16 as
required; No smoking; Parking 259
🛏 Rooms

Whether you are a golfer or not, sitting beside the most famous hole in the world of golf is sure to be a thrill. For those really not interested, the sea views will compensate, especially when accompanied by afternoon tea. In this traditional, even hallowed, setting, the last thing you might expect to find would be a newcomer calling self the Chocolate Afternoon Tea. But here

it is: chocolate scones, cakes, brownies, gateaux, éclairs and tartlets can all be relished along with strawberries and chocolate sauce, and even a choice of five chocolate-based cocktails. Traditionalists need not despair, for the cream tea is here too.

RECOMMENDED IN THE AREA
St Andrews Museum; British Golf Museum; St Andrews Deer Centre

*T*he Westin Turnberry Resort ★ ★ ★ ★ ★ ◎ ◎

Elaborate afternoon teas to take the mind off golf

☎ 01655 331000
🖷 01655 331706
📧 turnberry@westin.com
🌐 www.westin.com/turnberry

Map ref 9 - NS02

TURNBERRY, KA26 9LT
*From Glasgow take A 77/M77 south
towards Stranraer; 2m past
Kirkoswald, follow signs for A719
Turnberry village. Hotel 500 metres
on right.*
☕ Open daily; Tea served 2pm-5pm;
Booking possible; Set tea price(s)
Afternoon Tea £15.50, Champagne
Afternoon Tea £21.50; Seats 60;
Parking 421
🛏 221 Rooms D from £195

*T*his world-famous golfing resort hotel knows a thing or two about entertaining. From its magnificent location overlooking the Atlantic coastline, with 800 acres of beautiful grounds surrounding it, it offers the perfect retreat or leisure break. Golf is at its heart, and champions past, present and future have played the game here, and brought a wide following in their wake. One of the greatest pleasures of a visit, golfing or otherwise, is the afternoon tea served in the Ailsa lounge. French pastries and scones with clotted cream are all part of the package, with a choice of fine teas to accompany them.

RECOMMENDED IN THE AREA
Culzean Castle; Burns National Heritage Park; David Livingstone Centre

Iona

These hotels have told us that they offer afternoon tea to non-residents. Remember you may have to book, so please telephone in advance to avoid disappointment.

★ **Tigh an Eilean**
SHIELDAIG IV54 8XN
01520 755251
tighaneileanhotel@
shieldaig.fsnet.co.uk

★★ **Kilcamb Lodge Hotel**
STRONTIAN PH36 4HY
01967 402257
enquiries@kilcamblodge.co.uk

★★★ **Glenapp Castle**
BALLANTRAE
KA26 0NZ
01465 831212
enquiries@glenappcastle.com

★★★ **Kinloch House Hotel**
BLAIRGOWRIE
PH10 6SG
01250 884237
reception@kinlochhouse.com

★★★ **Kinnaird**
Kinnaird Estate
DUNKELD PH8 0LB
01796 482440
enquiry@kinnairdestate.com

★★★ **Ballathie House Hotel**
KINCLAVEN PH1 4QN
01250 883268
email@
ballathiehousehotel.com

★★★ **Inver Lodge Hotel**
LOCHINVER IV27 4LU
01571 844496
stay@inverlodge.com

★★★ **Cromlix House Hotel**
Kinbuck Nr
DUNBLANE FK15 9JT
01786 822125
reservations@
cromlixhouse.com

★★★ **Airds Hotel**
PORT APPIN PA38 4DF
01631 730236
airds@airds-hotel.com

★★★ **Rufflets Country House & Garden Restaurant**
Strathkinness Low Road
ST ANDREWS
KY16 9TX
01334 472594
reservations@rufflets.co.uk

★★★ **St Andrews Golf Hotel**
40 The Scores
ST ANDREWS
KY16 9AS
01334 472611
reception@
standrews-golf.co.uk

★★★ **Loch Torridon Country House Hotel**
By Achnasheen
Wester Ross
TORRIDON IV22 2EY
01445 791242
stay@lochtorridonhotel.com

★★★ **Lochgreen House Hotel**
Monktonhill Road
Southwood
TROON KA10 7EN
01292 313343
lochgreen@
costley-hotels.co.uk

★★★★ **Aberdeen Patio Hotel**
Beach Boulevard
ABERDEEN
AB24 5EF
01224 633339
info@patiohotels.com

★★★★ **Copthorne Hotel Aberdeen**
122 Huntly Street
ABERDEEN
AB10 1SU
01224 630404
reservations.aberdeen@
mill-cop.com

★★★★ **Macdonald Ardoe House**
South Deeside Road
Blairs
ABERDEEN AB12 5YP
01224 860600
ardoe@macdonald-hotels.co.uk

★★★★ **Norwood Hall Hotel**
Garthdee Road Cults
ABERDEEN
AB15 9FX
01224 868951
info@norwood-hall.co.uk

★★★★ **The Marcliffe at Pitfodels**
North Deeside Road
ABERDEEN AB15 9YA
01224 861000
enquiries@marcliffe.com

★★★★ **Macdonald Forest Hills Hotel & Resort**
Kinlochard
ABERFOYLE FK8 3TL
01877 387277
forest_hills@
macdonald-hotels.co.uk

★★★★ **Fairfield House Hotel**
12 Fairfield Road
AYR KA7 2AR
01292 267461
reservations@
fairfieldhotel.co.uk

★★★★ **Beardmore Hotel**
Beardmore Street
CLYDEBANK
G81 4SA
0141 951 6000
info@beardmore.scot.nhs.uk

★★★★ **The Westerwood Hotel**
1 St Andrews Drive
Westerwood
CUMBERNAULD
G68 0EW
01236 457171
westerwood@
morton-hotels.com

★★★★ **Macdonald Crutherland House**
Strathaven Road
EAST KILBRIDE
G75 0QZ
01355 577000
crutherland@
macdonald-hotels.co.uk

★★★★ **Carlton Hotel**
North Bridge
EDINBURGH EH1 1SD
0131 472 3000
carlton@
paramount-hotels.co.uk

★★★★ **Channings**
15 South Learmonth
Gardens
EDINBURGH EH4 1EZ
0131 332 3232
reserve@channings.co.uk

★★★★ **Edinburgh Marriott Hotel**
111 Glasgow Road
EDINBURGH EH12 8NF
0870 400 7293
edinburgh@
marriotthotels.co.uk

★ ★ ★ ★ Macdonald
Holyrood Hotel
Holyrood Road
EDINBURGH EH8 8AU
0131 550 4500
holyrood@
macdonald-hotels.co.uk

★ ★ ★ ★ Norton
House Hotel &
Restaurant
Ingliston
EDINBURGH EH28 8LX
0131 333 1275
nortonhouse-cro@
handpicked.co.uk

★ ★ ★ ★ Novotel
Edinburgh Centre
Lauriston Place
Lady Lawson Street
EDINBURGH EH3 9DE
0131 656 3500
H3271@accor.com

★ ★ ★ ★ Prestonfield
Priestfield Road
EDINBURGH EH16 5UT
0131 225 7800
reservations@prestonfield.com

★ ★ ★ ★ The
Howard Hotel
34 Great King Street
EDINBURGH EH3 6QH
0131 557 3500
reserve@thehoward.com

★ ★ ★ ★ The
Roxburghe Hotel
38 Charlotte Square
EDINBURGH EH2 4HG
0131 240 5500
roxburghe@
macdonald-hotels.co.uk

★ ★ ★ ★ Inverlochy
Castle Hotel
Torlundy
FORT WILLIAM
PH33 6SN
01397 702177
info@inverlochy.co.uk

★ ★ ★ ★ Cally
Palace Hotel
GATEHOUSE OF FLEET
DG7 2DL
01557 814341
info@callypalace.co.uk

★ ★ ★ ★ Langs Hotel
Port Dundas Place
GLASGOW G2 3LD
0141 33 1500
reservations@langshotels.co.uk

★ ★ ★ ★ Millennium
Hotel Glasgow
George Square
GLASGOW G2 1DS
0141 332 6711
reservations.glasgow@
mill-cop.com

★ ★ ★ ★ Radisson
SAS Glasgow
301 Argyle Street
GLASGOW G2 8DL
0141 204 3333
reservations.glasgow@
radissonsas.com

★ ★ ★ ★ Culloden
House Hotel
Culloden INVERNESS
IV2 7BZ
01463 790461
reserv@cullodenhouse.co.uk

★ ★ ★ ★ Balbirnie
House
Balbirnie Park
MARKINCH KY7 6NE
01592 610066
reservations@balbirnie.co.uk

★ ★ ★ ★ Macdonald
Cardrona Hotel Golf
& Country Club
Cardrona Mains
PEEBLES EH45 6LZ
01896 831144
general.cardrona@
macdonald-hotels.co.uk

★ ★ ★ ★ Peebles
Hotel Hydro
PEEBLES EH45 8LX
01721 720602
info@peebleshydro.com

★ ★ ★ ★ Macdonald
Inchyra Grange Hotel
Grange Road
POLMONT FK2 0YB
01324 711911
inchyra@
macdonald-hotels.co.uk

★ ★ ★ ★ Macdonald
Rusacks Hotel
Pilmour Links
ST ANDREWS
KY16 9JQ
0870 400 8128
general.rusacks@
macdonald-hotels.co.uk

★ ★ ★ ★ Highland
Hotel
Spittal Street
STIRLING FK8 1DU
01786 272727
stirling@
paramount-hotels.co.uk

★ ★ ★ ★ North West
Castle Hotel
STRANRAER DG9 8EH
01776 704413
info@northwestcastle.co.uk

★ ★ ★ ★ Macdonald
Houstoun House
UPHALL EH52 6JS
01506 853831
houstoun@
macdonald-hotels.co.uk

★ ★ ★ ★ ★ The
Gleneagles Hotel
AUCHTERARDER
PH3 1NF
01764 662231
resort.sales@gleneagles.com

★ ★ ★ ★ ★ The
Balmoral Hotel
1 Princes Street
EDINBURGH EH2 2EQ
0131 556 2414
reservations@
thebalmoralhotel.com

★ ★ ★ ★ ★
The Scotsman
20 North Bridge
EDINBURGH EH1 1YT
0131 556 5565
reservations@
thescotsmanhotelgroup.co.uk

★ ★ ★ ★ ★ The
Sheraton Grand
Hotel & Spa
1 Festival Square
EDINBURGH EH3 9SR
0131 229 9131
grandedinburgh.sheraton@
sheraton.com

Wales

Chief among teatime savouries in Wales must be the ever-popular Welsh rarebit: hot toast topped with a thickened sauce made from sharp cheese and local ale. Laverbread, edible seaweed, is another Welsh speciality, which can be cooked in butter and lemon juice and served on toast. Laverbread mixed with oatmeal is fried into little cakes, which are sometimes eaten at breakfast. In coastal areas you will also encounter cockles and mussels as a local delicacy. Cawl cennin, leek soup, is a great favourite, the leek being the Welsh national emblem. Leeks also combine well with the creamy local cheeses to make a tasty savoury tart. Caerphilly cheese, known locally as 'the crumblies', is mild and tangy and was traditionally favoured by miners for their lunch boxes. Among the tea breads are bara brith, a yeasted fruit bread, baked as a loaf and served sliced with

butter – available in all good tea shops – and Welsh cakes, a kind of scone, mixed quite stiff in this case to achieve a firm consistency, and fried on a griddle or frying pan. Welsh curd cakes are pastry tartlets filled with a mixture of junket, cake crumbs, butter, sugar and a few currants. Snowden pudding is a steamed suet pudding capped with raisins, which for special occasions might be accompanied by a wine sauce.

*G*walia Tea Rooms

Authentic tea room serving Welsh speciality foods

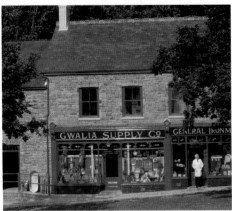

☎ 029 2056 6985
🖷 029 2058 6985

Map ref 2 - ST17

The Museum of Welsh Life, St Fagens, CARDIFF, CF5 6XB
Owner(s): Mike Morton
🍵 Open daily; Tea served 10am-4.45pm; Closed 24-25 Dec, 1 Jan; Booking possible; Set tea price(s) £5; Visa & Mastercard only; Seats 36; No smoking

A fascinating museum of Welsh life through the ages is the setting for this atmospheric tea room decorated and furnished in authentic 1920s style. Many of the buildings which form part of the museum have been moved stone by stone from all over Wales, and one such is the old general store which houses the Gwalia. Bentwood chairs, an etched glass screen and old photographs set the scene for the traditional tea menu, with its home-made cakes, and local specialities like Welsh rarebit, Teisen Lap (light and spicy fruit cake), Gwalia rock cake, and an excellent selection of speciality teas.

RECOMMENDED IN THE AREA
Museum of Welsh Life; Cardiff Castle; Llandaff Cathedral

Snowdonia National Park

*B*adgers Café & Patisserie

Llandudno's legendary tea room and patisserie located among the town centre shops

☎ 01492 871649
✉ manager@badgersgroup.co.uk
🌐 www.badgersgroup.co.uk

Map ref 5 - SH78

The Victoria Centre, Mostyn Street,
LLANDUDNO, LL30 2RP
Owner(s): Barry Mortlock
🍵 Open daily; Tea served 9.30am-5pm
Mon-Sat, 11am-4pm Sun; Closed Easter
Sun, 25-26 Dec, 1 Jan; Set tea price(s)
£5.25, £12.50; Seats 70; No smoking;
Air con

Conveniently located in the main shopping area of Llandudno, with a multi-storey car park close at hand, Badgers is the perfect place to rest, refuel and recuperate during a serious shopping expedition. The town's Victorian traditions are upheld, with waitresses – known as Badgers' Nippies – dressed in period costume. Regional specialities include Welsh rarebit, Welsh cakes, Welsh cheese salads, and bara brith, and home-roasted meats are featured among the sandwich fillings. There are two set teas: Welsh Cream Tea with scones, jam and cream and bara brith; and – the ultimate treat – Victorian Tea with a sandwich, bara brith, scones with jam and cream, and cake. All the cakes at Badgers are home made in the bakery upstairs, including patisserie items such as swan meringues, dragon éclairs and ice mice. A cake boxing service is also available. A harpist occasionally entertains the customers.

The Tea Guild's Award of Excellence 2005

RECOMMENDED IN THE AREA
*Bodnant Gardens; Snowdonia National Park;
Victorian Tramway to summit of Great Orme*

*O*sborne House ★★★★ ⊕

Beautifully renovated Victorian town house in a popular resort setting

☎ 01492 860330
🖷 01492 860791
📧 sales@osbornehouse.com
🌐 www.osbornehouse.com

Map ref 5 - SH78

17 North House, LLANDUDNO, LL30 2LP
A55 junct 19, follow signs to Llandudno, then Promenade. Left at War Memorial, then right; Osborne House on left opposite pier entrance.
🍴 Open daily; Tea served 3.30pm-5.30pm; Closed 17-30 Dec 2006; Booking possible; Set tea price(s) Welsh Tea £6, Full Afternoon Tea £8.25, Champagne Tea £35 for two people; Seats 70; No smoking in restaurant; Air con; Guide dogs only
🛏 6 Rooms

*L*ovingly transformed over a number of years, this impressive all-suite hotel has retained much of its period character. The marbled entrance hall, Victorian fireplaces, ornate ceilings and sparkling chandeliers provide the backdrop for some fine antique pieces and original artwork. Afternoon tea is served in the lounge area or café, and there are a couple of tables outside for fine weather. Options at tea time are the traditional version with a cucumber sandwich, scone, jam and cream, or the Champagne Tea for two people comprising smoked salmon sandwich, scone, jam and cream with half a bottle of champagne. Light bites and main meals are also available. Older children welcome.

RECOMMENDED IN THE AREA

Bodnant Gardens; Conwy and Caernarfon Castles; Llandudno Pier, Promenade and Marine Drive

Bara Brith (Welsh speckled fruit bread)

Recipe supplied by Osborne House
(page 178)

Ingredients

6oz (175g) currants
6oz (175g) sultanas
8oz (225g) light brown sugar
10oz (275g) self raining flour
¾ pint (500ml) strong tea
1 egg

Method

Soak currants and sultanas in the tea overnight.
Add to the sugar, flour and egg.
Pour into a loaf tin and bake at gas mark 6/400°F/200°C for
approximately 35 minutes.

St Tudno
Hotel and Restaurant ★★ ◉◉

Beautiful hotel with fine sea views

☎ 01492 874411
🖷 01492 860407
📧 sttudnohotel@btinternet.com
🌐 www.st-tudno.co.uk

Map ref 5 - SH78

The Promenade, LLANDUDNO,
LL30 2LP
On promenade, opposite pier.
🍴 Open daily; Tea served
2.30pm-5pm; Booking recommended
for large groups; Set tea price(s)
£10.95-£21.95; Seats 45; Smoking
area available; Dogs allowed at
manager's discretion; Parking 12;
🛏 19 Rooms

*A*fternoon tea doesn't come much better than this. The teas served at this lovely hotel could be judged as excellent by the extent of the afternoon tea menu, with pages of tempting choices. But the proof of the pudding is in the eating, and the St Tudno's choices are truly delicious. The Traditional Welsh tea and the Deluxe selection come with a pot of loose-leaf speciality tea from around 14 classic choices: from India there's Assam and Darjeeling, from Sri Lanka you'll find Uva and Ceylon, and the four representatives of China are Formosa Lapsang Souchong, Gunpowder, and Keemun. There are separate lists of sandwiches, savouries, home made cakes and strawberries and cream. The welcome is friendly, and the lounge with its glorious sea views is most inviting.

RECOMMENDED IN THE AREA
Bodnant Gardens; Conwy Castle; Great Orme Copper Mines

*L*langoed Hall ★★★★ ◉◉

Creeper-clad Jacobean/Edwardian great house

☎ 01874 754525
🖷 01874 754545
✉ enquiries@llangoedhall.com
🌐 www.llangoedhall.com

Map ref 2 - SO13

LLYSWEN, LD3 0YP
On A470 between Brecon and Builth Wells.
Owner(s): Mr C C Milne
☕ Open daily; Tea served weekdays 2pm-5pm, weekends 3pm-5pm; Booking possible; Set tea price(s) £8-£14.50; Seats 40; Smoking area available; No dogs; Children over the age of 8, and babies welcome; Parking 80; 🛏 23 Rooms

*T*he Welsh Parliament once stood on this spot, and the great country house that is now Llangoed Hall is suitably impressive. Tea is served in the gracious lounge, the bright garden room, the cheerful morning room, and the grand library itself. Turn up any afternoon for the cream tea, and enjoy scones, clotted cream, jam and Welsh cakes. Twenty-four hours' notice is required for the speciality full afternoon tea, but it is well worth planning in advance.

RECOMMENDED IN THE AREA

Hay-on-Wye bookshops; Brecon Beacons National Park; Hereford Cathedral and Mappa Mundi

Llangoed Griddle Blueberry Scones

Recipe supplied by Llangoed Hall
(page 181)

Ingredients

1lb (450g) self raising flour
4oz (110g) butter
6oz (175g) blueberries
3½oz (100g) caster sugar
2 eggs
2–4 tablespoons milk

Method

Sift flour, them rub in butter. Fold in currants, sultanas, blueberries and sugar. Make a well in the centre and add the eggs, 2 tablespoons of the milk and mix to a soft dough. If it feels too dry, add the remaining 2 tablespoons of milk.

Roll out the dough ½in (1cm) thick on a floured surface and cut into 2½in (6cm) rounds using a scone cutter.

Warm a frying pan to a medium heat and cook the scones in a little butter for 4–5 minutes until golden brown. They are best served warm.

Cemlyn
Restaurant & Tea Shop

Centrally located in Harlech's High Street-a tea shop by day and a restaurant by night

☎ 01766 780425
🌐 www.cemlynrestaurant.co.uk

Map ref 5 - SH53

High Street, HARLECH, LL46 2YA
In town centre on B4573, between Post Office & chemist's shop.
Owner(s): Jan & Geoff Cole
☕ Open Tue-Sun 10am-5pm, Easter to end Oct; Tea served all day; Closed Mon except Bank Hols Nov-Feb; Booking essential for 'Cemlyn Upstairs' but not for main tea room; Set tea price(s) £4.50-£22.50; Seats 30; No smoking; Dogs allowed on terrace; Children welcome in ground floor tea room

A tea shop and restaurant with rooms, Cemlyn is happily situated to provide views of Harlech's 13th-century castle, Royal St David's Golf Course, the mountains and the sea. Both cigarettes and tea bags are banned from this no-smoking, all-tea leaf establishment, which makes an uncompromising commitment to quality. An eclectic choice of teas, tisanes and infusions is offered alongside home-made brownies, tea cakes, scones and regional favourites such as Welsh cakes and bara brith. Light lunches are served and even the sandwiches are made with home-made bread. A patio area is provided for outdoor seating in fine weather, and bed and breakfast accommodation is available for guests wishing to sleep over. Tea, coffee, preserves, recipes and guidebooks are sold on the premises for customers to enjoy at home. Dogs are permitted outside on the patio.

The Tea Guild's Award of Excellence 2005

RECOMMENDED IN THE AREA
Harlech Castle; Lasynys Fawr; Welsh House; Snowdonia; National Park

These hotels have told us that they offer afternoon tea to non-residents. Remember you may have to book, so please telephone in advance to avoid disappointment.

★★ **Maes y Neuadd Country House Hotel**
TALSARNAU LL47 6YA
01766 780200
maes@neuadd.com

★★★ **Seiont Manor Hotel**
Llanrug CAERNARFON
LL55 2AQ
01286 673366
seiontmanor-cro@
handpicked.co.uk

★★★ **Ynyshir Hall**
EGLWYSFACH
SY20 8TA
01654 781209
ynyshir@relaischateaux.com

★★★ **Lake Country House Hotel**
LLANGAMMARCH
WELLS LD4 4BS
01591 620202
info@lakecountryhouse.co.uk

★★★★ **Coed-Y-Mwstwr Hotel**
Coychurch BRIDGEND
CF35 6AF
01656 860621
hotel@coed-y-mwstwr.com

★★★★ **Angel Hotel**
Castle Street CARDIFF
CF10 1SZ
029 2064 9200
angelreservations@
paramount-hotels.co.uk

★★★★ **Cardiff Marriott Hotel**
Mill Lane CARDIFF
CF10 1EZ
029 2039 9944
sara.nurse@
marriotthotels.co.uk

★★★★ **Copthorne Hotel Cardiff-Caerdydd**
Copthorne Way
Culverhouse Cross
CARDIFF CF5 6DH
029 2059 9100
sales.cardiff@mill-cop.com

★★★★ **Jurys Cardiff Hotel**
Mary Ann Street
CARDIFF CF10 2JH
029 2034 1441
info@jurysdoyle.com

★★★★ **Macdonald Holland House**
24/26 Newport Road
CARDIFF CF24 0DD
0870 122 0020
revenue.holland@
macdonald-hotels.co.uk

★★★★ **Novotel Cardiff Central**
Schooner Way
Atlantic Wharf
CARDIFF CF10 4RT
029 2047 5000
h5982@accor.com

★★★★ **Marriott St Pierre Hotel & Country Club**
St Pierre Park
CHEPSTOW NP16 6YA
01291 625261

★★★★
Parkway Hotel
Cwmbran Drive
CWMBRAN NP44 3UW
01633 871199
enquiries@parkwayhotel.co.uk

★★★★ **Vale Hotel Golf & Spa Resort**
Hensol Park
HENSOL CF72 8JY
01443 667800
reservations@vale-hotel.com

★★★★
Bodysgallen Hall
LLANDUDNO
LL30 1RS
01492 584466
info@bodysgallen.com

★★★★ **Morgans Hotel**
Somerset Place
SWANSEA SA1 1RR
01792 484848
info@morganshotel.co.uk

★★★★ **Swansea Marriott Hotel**
The Maritime Quarter
SWANSEA SA1 3SS
0870 400 7282

★★★★ **The Grand Hotel**
Ivey Place High Street
SWANSEA SA1 1NE
01792 645898
info@
thegrandhotelswansea.co.uk

★★★★★ **The St David's Hotel & Spa**
Havannah Street
CARDIFF CF10 5SD
029 2045 4045
reservations@
thestdavidshotel.com

★★★★★ **The Celtic Manor Resort**
Coldra Woods
NEWPORT NP18 1HQ
01633 413000
postbox@celtic-manor.com

Index

Credits

The Automobile Association wishes to thank the following photo
libraries for their assistance in the preparation of this book.

Bananastock 13, 47, 49, 56, 70, 90b, 124, 129b, 140, 144, 147, 157, 159,
167, 172; Photodisc 44, 53, 61, 78, 90t, 92, 99, 115, 129t, 134, 181, 183;
AA World Travel Library/Jeff Beazley 177r; Malc Birkitt 35, 37, 56r;
Michael Busselle 79; Nick Channer 148; Chris Coe 81; Rick Czaja 122r;
Steve Day 49, 67, 68, 109, 142, 170; Derek Forss 132, 174; Paul Grogan
112; Mike Haywood 120; Anthony Hopkins 135; Nick Jenkins 177l;
Caroline Jones 58r, 64, 122l, 178; Max Jourdan 88; Andrew Lawson 4;
Cameron Lees 40, 111; Tom Mackie 110, 128; S & O Mathews 118, 136,
138; Simon McBride 103; Andrew Midgley 56l; Rich Newton 112; Ken
Paterson 168; Hugh Palmer 75, 141; Clive Sawyer 131; Barrie Smith 62,
100; Tony Souter 34, 72; Jon Sparks 56; Richard Surman 76; Michael
Taylor 163r; Rupert Tenison 41; James Tims 84; Richard Turpin 106;
Wyn Voysey 65; Jonathan Welsh 127; Stephen Whitehorne 163l; Linda
Whitwam 38, 162; Harry Williams 59; Peter Wilson 12, 82.

Why not search online?

Visit **www.theAA.com** and search around 8000 inspected and rated hotels and B&Bs in Great Britain and Ireland. Then contact the establishment direct by clicking the 'Make a Booking' button...

...it's as easy as that!

Whatever your preference, we have the place for you. From a farm cottage to a city centre hotel — we have them all.

AA

Readers' Report form

Please send this form to:
AA Lifestyle Guides
The Automobile Association
Fanum House
Basingstoke RG21 4EA
or fax: (01256) 491647
or e-mail: lifestyleguides@theAA.com

If you've enjoyed Afternoon Tea at a teashop, tea room or in a hotel not recommended in this guide, why not tell us about it?

Please note, however, that if you have a complaint to make during a visit, we strongly recommend that you discuss the matter with the establishment management there and then so that they have a chance to put things right before your visit is spoilt. The AA does not undertake to arbitrate between you and the establishment, or to obtain compensation or engage in correspondence.

Date:

Your name (block capitals)

Your address (block capitals)

....

....

....

.... e-mail address:

Comments (please include the name and address of the establishment)

....

....

....

....

....

....

(please attach a separate sheet if necessary)

We may use information we hold about you to write, e-mail or telephone you about other services offered by us and our carefully selected partners.

Please tick here if you DO NOT wish to receive details of other products or services from the AA

Have you bought any other AA Britain's Best guides or other accommodation, restaurant, pub, or food guides recently? If yes, which ones?

....

....

Why did you buy the guide? To find a place for tea...

    For a celebration   On holiday   While shopping

    Break while travelling   other..

How often do you visit a place for tea? (circle one choice)

    more than once a month   once a month   once in 2-3 months

    once in six months   once a year   less than once a year

Please answer these questions to help us make improvements to the guide:

Which of these factors are most important when choosing a place for tea?

    Price   Location   Awards/ratings   Service

    Decor/surroundings   Previous experience   Recommendation

Other (please state): ....

Do you read the editorial features in the guide? ....

Do you use the location atlas? ....

Which elements of the guide do you find the most useful when choosing somewhere to have tea?

    Description   Photo   Rating

Can you suggest any improvements to the guide?

....

....

....

Readers' Report form

Please send this form to:
> AA Lifestyle Guides
> The Automobile Association
> Fanum House
> Basingstoke RG21 4EA
> or fax: (01256) 491647
> or e-mail: lifestyleguides@theAA.com

If you've enjoyed Afternoon Tea at a teashop, tea room or in a hotel not recommended in this guide, why not tell us about it?

Please note, however, that if you have a complaint to make during a visit, we strongly recommend that you discuss the matter with the establishment management there and then so that they have a chance to put things right before your visit is spoilt. The AA does not undertake to arbitrate between you and the establishment, or to obtain compensation or engage in correspondence.

Date:

Your name (block capitals)

Your address (block capitals)

....

....

....

.... e-mail address:

Comments (please include the name and address of the establishment)

....

....

....

....

....

....

(please attach a separate sheet if necessary)

We may use information we hold about you to write, e-mail or telephone you about other services offered by us and our carefully selected partners.

Please tick here if you DO NOT wish to receive details of other products or services from the AA

Readers' Report form

Have you bought any other AA Britain's Best guides or other accommodation, restaurant, pub, or food guides recently? If yes, which ones?

....

....

Why did you buy the guide? To find a place for tea...

For a celebration   On holiday   While shopping

Break while travelling   other..

How often do you visit a place for tea? (circle one choice)

more than once a month   once a month   once in 2-3 months

once in six months   once a year   less than once a year

Please answer these questions to help us make improvements to the guide:

Which of these factors are most important when choosing a place for tea?

Price   Location   Awards/ratings   Service

Decor/surroundings   Previous experience   Recommendation

Other (please state): ....

Do you read the editorial features in the guide? ....

Do you use the location atlas? ....

Which elements of the guide do you find the most useful when choosing somewhere to have tea?

Description   Photo   Rating

Can you suggest any improvements to the guide?

....

....

....